Fascism in America and the 28th Amendment
Second Edition

Eric Michael Moberg

Dedicated to freedom fighters everywhere

Academy Press
Salamanca, Ontario, San Francisco, Bologna

See author's Academia page at:
https://sfsu.academia.edu/EricMoberg

and his Amazon page at:
https://www.amazon.com/ s?ie=UTF8&page=1&rh=n%3A283155%2Cp_27%3AEric%20Moberg

or his Goodreads page at:
https://www.goodreads.com/author/show/4953962.Eric_Michael_Moberg

ISBN-13: 978-1974034994

ISBN-10: 1974034992

Cover photo "Political Prisoner" by Pedro Ribeiro Simões

Table of Contents

Introduction

"Every man would be a tyrant if we let him."
—Abigail Adams

"In certain contingencies violence has a deep moral significance."
—Benito Mussolini

"Fascism is capitalism plus murder."
—Upton Sinclair

Fascism in name begins with Mussolini at the end of World War I in the Italy of Caligula, Dante, Machiavelli, and the Holy Roman Church that would made common cause with Mussolini,[1] and Social scientists began to label Benito Mussolini a Machiavellian as early as 1929.[2] The roots of nationalism, militarism, expansionism, and authoritarianism in the United States surround and predate the founding of our republic. As Fox News warned us, in a somewhat hyperbolic 2009 comparison of President Obama to Mussolini, Mussolini laughed off calls for socialism or liberal democracy, such as the U.S. Constitution promises, and proceeded to enact and execute his ideology and tactics to reshape Italy during the 1920s to 1940s:

> Democracy is talking itself to death. The people do not know what they want; they do not know what is the best for them. There is too much foolishness, too much lost motion. I have

---

[1] David Kertzer, *The Pope and Mussolini: The Secret History of Pius XI and the Rise of Fascism in Europe,* (New York: Random House, 2014).
[2] Arnold J. Lien, "Machiavelli's Prince and Mussolini's Facism," *Social Science* 4, no. 4 (1929): 435-41, http://www.jstor.org/stable/23902033.

stopped the talk and the nonsense. I am a man of action. Democracy is beautiful in theory; in practice it is a fallacy. You in America will see that someday.[3]

In the Americas, slavery was common among various tribes subduing enemies as well as the Spanish conquistadors enslaving the indigenous before and after the arrival of the pilgrims.[4] In the United States, the founders, many of whom owned slaves, rejected the authoritarianism of the monarch King George, and George Washington clearly stated from the start that he would agree to serve as first president but would not accept anointment as king or even run for a third term—though he was in perfect health and more popular than ever.[5] Yet, many historians and commentators have noted the steady growth of powers in the American presidency, especially in the 20th century,[6] leading to what we should describe as a dangerous American style of authoritarianism,[7] a Corporate-Fascism that requires limits that the legislature and the courts seem unable or unwilling to enforce.[8]

In the wake of the 2016 election of Donald Trump, various individuals began reading such cautionary tales as *The Plot Against America, 1984, The Handmaid's Tale,* and *It Can't Happen Here.* Journalists such as Natasha Lennard began to us

---

[3] Tommy De Seno, "Beware Obama's Road to Serfdom," Fox News, 17 March 2009.

[4] Andrés Reséndez, *The Other Slavery: The Uncovered Story of Indian Enslavement in America,* (New York: Houghton Mifflin Harcourt, 2016).

[5] David Boaz, "The Man Who Would Not Be King," *Cato Institute*, 20 February 2006. https://www.cato.org/publications/commentary/man-who-would-not-be-king.

[6] Bruce Ackerman, *The Decline and Fall of the American Republic,* (Cambridge: Belknap Press, 2013).

[7] Robert Dalleck, "Power and the Presidency, from Kennedy to Obama," *Smithsonian Magazine*, January 2011.

[8] Dana Nelson, "The Growth of Executive Power Has Turned Politics into War," *Washington Post*, 8 March 2016.

the "F" word openly, writing on the eve of the Trump
inauguration:

> □We *can* deploy the "fascism" moniker to Trump's
> ascendance by recognizing features like selective populism,
> nationalism, racism, traditionalism, the deployment of
> Newspeak and disregard for reasoned debate. The reason
> we *should* use the term is because, taken together, these
> aspects of Trumpism are not well combated or contained by
> standard liberal appeals to reason. It is constitutive of its
> fascism that it demands a different sort of opposition.[9]

Others have eschewed books and essays to form resistance
groups, including Refuse Fascism, and the more militant Antifa.
Mitch McConnell's April 2017 threats to alter the
longstanding 60-vote cloture rule to end debate on the Senate's
Constitutional advise-and-consent role in selecting Supreme
Court justices[10] was only the latest echo of Mussolini's fascist
philosophy in American politics. George W. Bush repeatedly
mocked the United Nations in 2003 as an irrelevant[11] debating
society when they would not rubber stamp his proposed
resolutions to wage war on Iraq. President Obama ignored all the
public talk and desire for the public option when pressing his
signature healthcare legislation, excusing this betrayal in a 2016
Journal of American Medical Association as "unrealistic."[12]
What Obama's pragmatic approach acknowledges is that the will

---

[9] Natasha Lennard, "Anti-Fascists Will Fight Trump's Fascism in the Streets:
In Stark Contrast with Many Liberals, Antifa Activists Refuse Any Dialogue
with Trumpism," *The Nation*, 19 January 2017.

[10] Clare Foran, "The 'Nuclear Option' Won't Dramatically Change the
Senate," *The Atlantic*, 4 April 2017.

[11] Maura Reynolds and Paul Richter, "Bush Says U.N. Must Act or Be
'Irrelevant,'" *Los Angeles Times*, 14 February 2003.

[12] James Capreta, "On Obamacare, The President Ignores Unpleasant
Realities," *National Review*, 15 July 2016.

of the people—no matter how clear or strong or sensible—is irrelevant when it contradicts the will of corporate establishment. And healthcare is only one example that reveals the "fallacy" of democracy in the United States.

Wall Street lusts over profits from war, so the world suffers endless wars. Wall Street envisions profits from private prisons, so Geo and other corrections corporations secure contracts with states guaranteeing an uninterrupted flow of inmates and the advantage of paying private guards a fraction of what government employees earn at state facilities so as to maximize profits. Corporate CEOs covet exorbitant salaries and bonuses, so boards of directors ignore workers' needs for a living wage and pay top executives as much as 500-times more than workers, while Congress stalls minimum-wage legislation for years. Finance and corporations want to subvert any power that labor can marshal to resist hierarchy, so legislatures at the state and federal level enact laws written by ALEC and similar extremely pro-business institutions to destabilize workers, reduce their rights, and create a timid proletariat that management can dismiss summarily and arbitrarily as individuals or abandon as groups by moving a business to a friendlier city, state, or nation, leaving workers in what Trotsky described as a state of "dispersion and helplessness," just as Mussolini sought as early as 1921: "Thus understood, Fascism, is totalitarian, and the Fascist State—a synthesis and a unit inclusive of all values—interprets, develops, and potentates the whole life of a people."[13]

From the establishment of Fascism, alternatives have existed. Gramsci and the Italian Communist Party posed such a real competition to Mussolini and his Fascist Party that Mussolini manipulated the arrest and imprisonment of Gramsci. The Italian

---

[13] Benito Mussolini, *The Doctrine of Fascism*, (Rome: Ardita Publishing, 1935), Kindle locations 107.

Communists offered a vision that was less violent, less empirical, less xenophobic, less hierarchical, and much less totalitarian than the Fascist vision that Mussolini eventually imposed. Had London and Wall Street bankers not financed the rise of Hitler, the United States would not have needed to enter World War II. Had Britain and France negotiated the Treaty of Versailles more reasonably, there would have been much less despair and alienation in Germany for Hitler to manipulate. Had Roosevelt not interfered with the gas supplies of the Japanese, Hirohito would have had no reason to order the attack on the fleet at Pearl Harbor. The dropping of the atomic bombs in Hiroshima and Nagasaki were not only vicious but entirely unnecessary according to military strategists prosecuting the war. The U.S. wars on Korea and Vietnam were immoral and unnecessary from any true national security consideration, and the American people gained nothing from them, to say nothing of the millions of casualties amongst the Korean and Vietnamese. The War on Drugs has done little or nothing to curb drug abuse, though it has destroyed millions of lives through draconian incarceration and violence by militarized police. The War on Terror has only exacerbated the state violence and spread terrorism all over the globe, creating terrorists where none had previously existed. The state then cites the new terrorists as cause for more military assaults in foreign lands, causing desperation that is fertile territory for terrorist response, thus continuing a cycle of perpetual terrorism and war—official state terrorism. Meanwhile, back in the United States, the government continues to eviscerate constitutional freedoms in the name of national security; the freedom of the press or freedom from unwarranted searches mean little in the age of omnipresent state surveillance and complicit judges recommended by such dark and authoritarian organizations as the Federalist Society, funded by authoritarian corporate power brokers.

The circumstances call for a radical, revolutionary response that must include a cultural and societal awakening that we are beginning to see in the many protests of 2016 and 2017; we also need a 28th Amendment to curb corporate power and influence on our elected representatives, who rarely even consider, let alone obey, the will or good of the people. And, at the same time, as Jane McAlvey urges, we must organize ourselves with millions of other ordinary people to transfer power from elites to the majority so that we can analyze the circumstances, set the goals, design the strategy, and pursue our own success.[14]

---

[14] Jane F. McAlevey, *No Shortcuts: Organizing for Power in the New Gilded Age,* (Oxford: Oxford University Press, 2017), 10.

The State

Mussolini proclaimed from his balcony overlooking Rome to a crowd of more than 200,000 people that he had reinstated the glorious empire on the fateful hills of Rome."[15] His concept of the Fascist State in its "corporative conception" sought to place citizens into whatever productive work the government decided was most valuable.[16] The nation needed workers and warriors, not voters. Though Mussolini claimed that his was a third way—not capitalist nor communist, but Fascist—the so called corporate state in reality tipped the balance of power toward capital as soon as it banned strikes and unions that wer not sanctioned by the Fascist government itself. In 1922, soon after ascending to power by invitation of the King, Mussolini wrote in the second edition of the monthly review he launched, *Gerarchia*, that the liberal and democratic principles of 1789 had failed and new aristocracies were emerging that required opposition by an authoritarian, totalitarian state. Five years later, in his famous Ascension Day speech in May of 1927, he declared that any

---

[15] Simona Colarizi cited in Neelam Srivastava, Neelam, "Anti-Colonialism and the Italian Left," *Interventions: The International Journal of Postcolonial Studies* 8, no. 3: 419.

[16] Benito Mussolini, *My Autobiography*, (Mineola, New York: Dover, 2006), Kindle locations 2560-2562.

"opposition is silly, superfluous in a totalitarian regime like the Fascist regime...."[17] The next year, his autobiography went further and in more poetic prose: "Our love of country had bloomed again," celebrating a unification in which all Italians "felt our formidable weight in the future of a new Europe," in which new "generations of Italians rejoiced, for the Italian cities were once again rejoined to the country," just as "Dante had prophesied and defined in the fourteenth century."[18] Mussolini created his twentieth-century interpretation of Dante's vision with the infamous show of force that came to be known as the March on Rome, when the Fascists "had mobilized three hundred thousand black shirts," of which were "sixty thousand armed men ready for action."[19] The resulting "negotiations carried on with unwavering constancy," in the parliament, capital, and country when Mussolini ultimately "united Italian Nationalism with Fascism," thus creating a one-party, totalitarian and authoritarian state that would define Fascism for future generations and iterations.[20]

While the United States had, prior to 1923, and has since laid claim to multi-party democratic rule, the two major parties rarely differ significantly on matters of empire.[21] When the state wants expansion through Manifest Destiny or thinly veiled wars of empire, Whig, Bull Moose, Democratic, and Republican leaders typically fall in line.[22] Neither can the individual citizen expect much protection from any party leaders against overzealous law enforcement authorities at the local or national level; both major

---

[17] Nicholas Farrell, *Mussolini: A New Life*, (London: Endeavour Press, 2015), Kindle locations 4618-4619.

[18] Mussolini, *My Autobiography*, Kindle locations 2560-2562.

[19] Ibid., Kindle locations 1750-1753.

[20] Ibid., Kindle locations 1927-1932.

[21] Nader, Ralph, *Crashing the Party,* (New York: MacMillan, 2007).

[22] Andrew J. Bacevich, *The New American Militarism: How Americans Are Seduced by War,* (Oxford: Oxford University Press, 2005).

parties regularly vote nearly unanimously to fund the national security state, the surveillance state, and the carceral state that profit America's own version of the corporate state.[23] As veteran journalist and Pulitzer Prize winner Chris Hedges laments, "the individual citizen has become irrelevant."[24] Whereas Mussolini contained industry within the state, industry—particularly the finance sector—has captured the state and all its functions in the 21st century United States, effectively moving the real seat of power from Washington D. C. to Wall Street, with occasional vacations in Davos or the Cayman Islands.[25] When the occasional brave politician dares challenge Wall Street hegemony, such as Franklin Delano Roosevelt did with his New Deal project, the American Corporate-Fascists respond, as they did in 1933 with a coup plot that included wealthy industrialists such as the Rockefellers, wealthy bankers such as J. P. Morgan, and thugs from the Ku Klux Klan.[26] Corporate-Fascism in the United States is in some ways more pernicious than Italian Fascism was in that the perpetrators of American authoritarianism and totalitarianism regularly mask their anti-democratic actions with secrecy or lies about threats, and the benefactors of American Corporate-Fascism are obscenely wealthy, private investors and corporations leveraging the treasury and the powers of the people to profit—not for the nation as a whole—but for the oligarchs alone.[27]

---

[23] Norman Solomon, *War Made Easy: How Presidents and Pundits Keep Spinning Us to Death*, (New York: The Disinformation Company, 2008).

[24] Christopher Hedges, *Wages of Rebellion: The Moral Imperative of Revolt*, (New York, Nation Books, 2015), 1.

[25] Larry Doyle, *In Bed with Wall Street: The Conspiracy Crippling Our Global Economy*, (Boston: St. Martin's Press, 2014).

[26] Jules Archer, *The Plot to Seize the White House: The Shocking True Story of the Conspiracy to Overthrow FDR*, (New York: Hawthorne Books, 1973).

[27] Noam Chomsky, *Profit Over People*, (New York: Seven Stories Press, 1998).

The founders worried openly about undue influence on the state by an "overbearing majority," as James Madison described in Federalist No. 10:

> Complaints are everywhere heard from our most considerate and virtuous citizens, equally the friends of public and private faith, and of public and personal liberty, that our governments are too unstable, that the public good is disregarded in the conflicts of rival parties, and that measures are too often decided, not according to the rules of justice and the rights of the minor party, but by the superior force of an interested and overbearing majority. However anxiously we may wish that these complaints had no foundation, the evidence, of known facts will not permit us to deny that they are in some degree true.

Madison, who would serve two terms as president, shows a concern for minority rights—the rights of rich white men, not the rights of slaves.[28] As recent scholars have noted, Madison's aversion to majority rule acts to "weaken ties between constituents and representations," while serving to "strengthen ties between representatives and politically privileged interest groups," because "elected representatives (and judges) tend to be well-off, highly educated, white males inclined to confuse their class interests with fundamental rights."[29] John Dewey issued a similar warning in 1932, observing that a

> genuine democracy will always secure to every individual a maximum of liberty of expression and will establish the conditions which will enable the minority by use of communication and persuasion to become a majority. The

---

[28] Paul Finkelman, "James Madison and the Bill of Rights: A Reluctant Paternity," *The Supreme Court Review* (1990).

[29] Mark A. Graber, "Conflicting Representations: Lani Guinier and James Madison on Electoral Systems," *Constitutional Commentary* 13, no. 3: 291.

real culprit is always some powerful minority which prefers to use methods of suppressive force or of perversion and degradation of opinion by means of propaganda. . . . The responsibility of the actual majority is not for originating the suppression but for standing passively by and permitting it to occur. Any fair-minded survey of suppressive acts in this country will demonstrate that their ultimate source is always a privileged minority.[30]

And the suppression and oppression in the United States continue through to the 21st century, mostly for the benefit for American Corporate-Fascist elites, including such greedy, unpatriotic, and reckless self-appointed plutocrats as Rex Tillerson, former Exxon-Mobil CEO and Trump Secretary of State. Tillerson faced bipartisan skepticism and opposition at the Senate confirmation hearings. Senator Rubio of Florida became frustrated with Tillerson's evasive answers on extrajudicial killings by Philippine President Duterte: "In order to achieve moral clarity," Rubio admonished, "we need clarity. We can't achieve moral clarity with rhetorical ambiguity." Tillerson was even more evasive when Senator Kaine of Virginia asked about climate change: Kaine complained "Do you lack the knowledge to answer my question or are you refusing to answer my question?" Tillerson persisted in defiance: "A little of both."[31] Senator Murphy of Connecticut argued that "There is no doubt Rex Tillerson is a successful businessman and a very smart person," but Tillerson has consistently shown a stubborn "willingness to put oil profits before national interests" so the idea of "handing him the keys of US foreign policy is a recipe for

---

[30] John Dewey, quoted in David Fott, "Dewey and the Threat of Tyranny of the Majority," *Perspectives on Political Science* 27, no. 4: 206.
[31] Cameron Joseph, "Tillerson Faces Rocky Secretary of State Confirmation Hearing as Rubio Hurls Tough Questions His Way," *New York Daily News*, 11 January 2017.

disaster."[32] As CEO, Tillerson "disparaged and downplayed the science on climate change, and his company is even currently under investigation under investigation for defrauding the public and shareholders for decades about the dangers of climate change caused by fossil fuels," according to Ken Kimmel, president of the Union of Concerned Scientists.[33] Yet some such as former Secretary of State Condoleezza Rice touted Tillerson's credentials and experience for the job, but after seven months on duty, Tillerson faced public ridicule in establishment publications such as *Foreign Policy*: "It's time to acknowledge that Tillerson is an abject failure, particularly in the area in which he was supposed to be best prepared," because he wrongly pursues a "robust American foreign policy," without recognizing "America's role as a real "force for universal" human and civil rights in a global economy and society.[34] But Rice and others should not be surprised, given Tillerson's long history of presiding over exploitation, corruption, and even torture by Exxon-Mobil, "it's hard to believe Tillerson wouldn't have had some idea of" the torture by "Exxon's Army" in Aceh, where the rampant "abuse was covered by news organizations—including the Associated Press and the *Wall Street Journal*—as early as the 1990s."[35] Abusing, exploiting, displacing, and torturing workers or dissidents is typical behavior for a Fascist state, in this case, the Great State of Exxon-Mobil.

In 1995, Umberto Eco, a former Fascist youth, outlined a list of features typical to what he referred to as Ur-Fascism or Eternal

---

[32] Ibid.

[33] Nicole Gaouette, "Why is Rex Tillerson As Secretary of State So Controversial?" CNN, 13 December 2017.

[34] Daniel B. Baer, "Condoleezza Rice and Bob Gates Should Apologize for Endorsing Rex Tillerson," *Foreign Policy*, 21 August 2017.

[35] Samantha Michaels, "Torture Allegations Shadow Rex Tillerson's Time at Exxon Mobil," *Mother Jones*, 11 January 2017.

Fascism.[36] Each and all apply historically and currently to the Corporate-Fascist State of the United States of America.

1. *Cult of Tradition*. We see calls to tradition in many ways, including frequent references to the Constitution, often by those who clearly have not read the document.[37] Racism, sexism, and paternalism in America invoke tradition in their defense, as does discrimination against those who reject gender or sexuality norms.[38]

2. *Rejection of Modernism*. American leaders who continue to deny evolution or climate disruption reject modernism.[39] The efforts in several states to force the inclusion of intelligent design or the exclusion of discussing the slave trade in the United States reject modern education.[40]

3. *Irrationalism and Action for Action's Sake*. Each of the U.S. military actions in Korea, Cuba, Vietnam, Grenada, Iraq, Afghanistan, Syria, and Yemen are irrational with respect of actual national security.[41] The Bush-Cheney mantra that we fight them there so we don't have to fight them here is not only irrational, given that there is no evidence for it, but the evidence and the simple logic contradict it; the more we attack other countries, the more likely we will inspire victims or their relatives to commit terrorism.[42]

---

[36] Umberto Eco, "Ur-Fascism," *New York Review of Books*, 22 June 1995.

[37] Michael Scherer, "Can President Trump Handle the Truth?," *Time*, 22 Mar 2017.

[38] Daniel Steinmetz-Jenkins and Brittany Pheiffer Noble, "Steve Bannon's Would-Be Coalition of Christian Traditionalists," *The Atlantic*, 23 March 2017.

[39] Zoe Schlanger, "Senator Inhofe Declares Kids 'Brainwashed' after Granddaughter Asks about Climate Change," *Newsweek*, 27 July 2016.

[40] Amanda Paulson, "Texas Textbook War: 'Slavery' or 'Atlantic Triangular Trade'?," *Christian Science Monitor*, 19 May 2010.

[41] Christopher Lane, "Why the Gulf War Was Not in the National Interest," *Atlantic Online*, July 1991.

[42] Brian Michael Jenkins, "Fifteen Years on, Where Are We in the 'War on

4. *Yes to Faith, No to Analytical Criticism.* When political rallies chant *USA-USA-USA* at a protestor who rises to question orthodoxy or doctrine, the chanters enforce faith and demonstrate a refusal to listen to criticism.[43] Similarly, Trump's demonization of the press and banning recordings of White House Press briefings show contempt for critical democratic engagement.[44]

5. *Consensus by Fear of Other.* The Nixon era Southern Strategy pits whites against blacks, which George H. W. Bush adapted in his notorious Willie Horton campaign ads denouncing Governor Dukakis as soft on crime.[45] The crime in this propaganda, of course, is always committed by blacks against whites.[46]

6. *Appeal to Frustration.* President Reagan promised a bright economic future for those middle class voters who were frustrated by rising gas prices and interest rates, but once in power, Reagan attacked labor unions.[47] President Clinton later promised a relief from rising crime rates through his signature crime bill, which actually led to the vast expansion of the prison population of many non-violent drug addicts.[48]

Terror'?," Rand Blog, 7 September 2016.

[43] Cindy Carcamo, Adam Elmahrek, and Ben Brazil "Violence Erupts at Pro-Trump rally in Huntington Beach," *Los Angeles Times*, 26 March 2017.

[44] Tom Kludt, "Off-camera, No Audio Broadcast: White House Keeps Undermining Press Briefing," CNN, 19 June 2017.

[45] Sam Tanehaus, "The Architect of the Radical Right: How the Nobel Prize–winning Economist James M. Buchanan Shaped Today's Antigovernment Politics," *The Atlantic*, July/August 2017.

[46] Ian Haney López, *Dog Whistle Politics: How Coded Racial Appeals Have Reinvented Racism and Wrecked the Middle Class*, (Oxford: Oxford University Press, 2013).

[47] Joseph A. McCartin, "The Strike That Busted Unions," *New York Times*, 2 August 2011.

[48] Julia Bowling, "The Crime Bill's Legacy, Two Decades Later," Brennan Center for Justice, 2 July 2014.

7. *Nationalism as Identity*. Trump's wall is the ultimate nationalist symbol.[49] His Muslim ban is more sophisticated in that whenever one of the world's over 1 billion followers of Islam commits an act of violence in the United States, Trump will blame his critics and rush to the Congress for new powers, as we saw with President George W. Bush and the un-Constitutional so called Patriot Act.[50]

8. *Direct Discontent Toward Wealthy Elites*. This is a difficult challenge for the Fascist forces in the United States, with all of their own wealth.[51] Their deceitful solution is to villainize groups such as nurses and teachers as somehow having too much political power or receiving too much pay or too many benefits, such as pensions, benefits that many American workers no longer expect for themselves.[52]

9. *No Struggle for Life: Life is for Struggle*. Endless wars for conquest and profit require both dehumanization of the victims in the targeted countries as well as a blind support of any violence committed by American military anywhere for any reason.[53] Peace activists are denounced as weak, or worse, traitors who should be jailed, exiled, or executed under laws such as the Alien and Sedition Act or the Espionage Act.[54]

---

[49] Rich Lowry, "The Nationalism Which Is So Repugnant to the Liberal Elite Seems Like Common Sense to Many Americans," *National Review*, 27 January 2017.

[50] Ryu Spaeth, "We're One Terrorist Attack Away from Donald Trump Doing Something Really Crazy," *New Republic*, 30 January 2017.

[51] David Choi, "'I Just Don't Want a Poor Person': Trump Explains Why He Added Billionaire Wall Street Execs to His Cabinet," *Business Insider*, 21 June 2017.

[52] John Bellamy Foster, "Public Sector Workers Are a 'Privileged New Class,' Says Billionaire," PBS, 17 January 2011.

[53] Sebastian Junger, "We're All Guilty of Dehumanizing the Enemy," *Washington Post*, 13 January 2012.

[54] "A New Front in the Legal Fight Over Donald Trump's Travel Ban," *Economist*, 23 June 2017.

10. *Reactionary Elitism.* American exceptionalism is almost universally accepted and unquestioned by any mainstream politician or member of the press.[55] Sarah Palin and Barak Obama both repeated the elitist phrase during the 2008 presidential campaign.[56] If Americans are special, they can ignore international norms, organizations, and laws.[57]

11. *Hero Worship.* Virtually every Hollywood police or military action movie features an underdog character who uses violence to save the day.[58] Often in police stories, a semi-rogue cop hero violates rules or laws to avenge honor or the death of a partner.[59]

12. *Sex as Violence.* It is not a coincidence that some of the most popular American video games allow players to commit unspeakable violence against scantily-clad and oversexualized female opponents.[60] The rape culture, too, rests largely on the objectification of female beauty and the fetishization of macho male strength or violence.[61]

13. *Selective Populism.* American democracy systematically excludes many would-be voters. The first method of exclusion is to limit citizenship.[62] The second is to exclude felons.[63] The third is to "cage" or suppress registration and

---

[55] "Is America Really Exceptional?," CNN, 12 September 2013.
[56] "American Exceptionalism: The Palin Version," *Economist*, 24 November 2010.
[57] Benjamin Wittes, *Legislating the War on Terror: An Agenda for Reform*, (Washington D. C.: Brookings Institution Press, 2010).
[58] Jenny McCartney, "The Brutal Truth About Violence in the Movies," *Telegraph*, 25 June 2013.
[59] Borys Kit, "Mel Gibson, Vince Vaughn Reteam for Thriller 'Dragged Across Concrete' (Exclusive)," *Hollywood Reporter*, 1 February 2017.
[60] "12 Horrifyingly Violent Video Games: History's Most Blood-Soaked and Gore-Spattered Releases," *Rolling Stone*, 11 October 2013.
[61] Arwa Mahdawi, "This is What Rape Culture Looks Like – in the Words of Donald Trump," *Guardian*, 15 October 2016.
[62] Jim Henson, "The Polling Center: GOP Voters and the Path to Citizenship," *Texas Tribune*, 21 March 2013.

actual voting of those who would likely oppose authoritarian candidates or support progressives.[64] When Clive Bundy used guns to threaten federal officials, the mainstream press portrayed him as a populist hero similar to Paul Revere.[65] When Philando Castile legally carried a handgun while driving his family to work, he was a dangerous drug abuser, and officer Jeronimo Yanez justified his murder by portraying Castile as unworthy of legal protection or status.[66]

14. *Newspeak.* Mitch McConnell attempted to sell the Republican effort to repeal Obamacare in terms of respecting "freedom" of Americans from mandates to buy health care that they, according to McConnell, do not need.[67]

The recent Texas anti-abortion laws similarly claimed to "protect" women's health, though the evidence presented in the related Supreme Court case demonstrated that the true intent and effects of the laws were to prevent women, prevent them from exercising the Constitutionally protected right to obtain abortion services.[68] President Trump's Muslim ban, which his surrogates reworded as a travel ban, claimed national security as its motivation.[69] Yet the evidence presented in the several ongoing

---

[63] K. K. Rebecca Lai and Jasmine C. Lee, "Why 10% of Florida Adults Can't Vote: How Felony Convictions Affect Access to the Ballot," *New York Times*, 6 October 2016.

[64] Nicol Turner-Lee, "Trump's Election Integrity Commission Needs to Redress Voter Suppression, Not Fraud," Brookings Institution, 21 June 2017.

[65] Chauncey Devega, "They'd Be Killed If They Were Black: The Racial Double Standard at the Heart of the New Bundy Family Standoff," *Salon*, 4 January 2016.

[66] Jelani Cobb, "Old Questions but No New Answers in the Philando Castile Verdict," *New Yorker,* 22 January 2017.

[67] Erica Werner, "Analysis: Health Bill Test of McConnell's Leadership Skills," ABC, 23 June 2017.

[68] Lindsey Cook, Kimberly Leonard, "Explaining the Whole *Woman's Health v. Hellerstedt* Abortion Case," *US News*, 11 January 2016.

[69] Matt Zapotosky, "Federal Appeals Court Rules 3 to 0 Against Trump on Travel Ban," *Washington Post*, 9 February 2017.

court battles has demonstrated that there exists no basis to show that Muslims, or travelers from the named countries, pose more threat than other travelers, to say nothing of the conspicuous absence of Saudi Arabia from the list of suspect countries, despite the long known connection of Saudi Arabia to the September 11 terrorist attacks.[70] But the American Corporate-Fascist State routinely ignores evidence and facts whenever they interfere with their own accumulation of wealth or power.

So what are the alternatives? What are the realistic and successful tactics, strategies, programs, and actions available to curb corporate power and force our elected representatives to obey the will of the vast majority of the people? Groups such as Our Revolution typically list the following issues as crucial to creating a progressive democracy:

- Reversing Catastrophic Climate Disruption
- Ending Hunger
- Establishing Affordable Housing for All
- Funding Free Medicare for All, including Prescriptions
- Reversing Climate Change
- Strengthening Social Security
- Reducing Income Inequality and College Tuition and Debt
- Exercising Cooperative Foreign Policy without War
- Reforming Immigration Policy
- Creating Decent Paying Jobs with at Least a Living Wage
- Creating Racial Justice and Ending Police Brutality
- Protecting Net Neutrality and Privacy
- Caring for Our Veterans

---

[70] Aryeh Neier, "Saudi Arabia and Egypt are excluded from Trump's ban. Why?," *Guardian*, 30 January 2017.

- Protecting Rights of Women, Tribal Nations, LGBT, those with AIDS or HIV, Persons with Disabilities, and Citizens of Puerto Rico

and perhaps the key to all reforms:

- Prohibiting Big Money in Politics[71]

The strategy must include both organizing each and every member of society and pursuing an intersectionality of progressive causes so that veterans support immigrants; persons with disabilities support LGBT, the wealthy help to end hunger, etc. The tactics must include efforts to create and further solidarity across progressive groups and causes in order to overcome forces that "implement the rules or fail to challenge" systems that encourage individuals and groups "to hate one another" in battles where the American Corporate-Fascist State watches and waits only to blame and punish victims while exonerating and rewarding instigators.[72]

---

[71] "Our Issues," Our Revolution, accessed 15 July 2017, https://ourrevolution.com/issues/.
[72] Patricia Hill Collins, "On Violence, Intersectionality and Transversal Politics," *Ethnic and Racial Studies*, 40:9, 1464, DOI: 10.1080/01419870.2017.1317827.

Philosophy

"Vain desires are always insatiable."
   —Epicurus

"Fascism, unique lighthouse in a sea of cowardice...."
   —Benito Mussolini

"We came, we saw, he died...[giggles]..."
   —Hillary Rodham Clinton

Mussolini wrote in his autobiography that he "wanted to create the impression of a complete and rigid consistence with an ideal," but without "a scheming...for personal gain," yet he knew "that once a man sets up to be the expounder of an idea or of a new school of thought," the man "must consistently and intensively live the daily life and fight battles for the doctrines that he teaches at any cost until victory-to the end!"[73] He celebrated war and idolized warriors,[74] especially the "impetuous" and "heroic" Italians who fought with "vigor and dash" in the numerous "city militias that flourished in many parts of Italy" and who "threw themselves into the battle with bombs in hands, with daggers in the teeth, with a supreme contempt for death," all the while "singing their magnificent war hymns," with not only a "sense of heroism but an indomitable will."[75] Indomitable "Fascism is" always only "a unit" for Mussolini, one that "cannot have varying tendencies and trends, as it cannot have two leaders on any one level of organization," for Fascism must always respect

---

[73] Mussolini, *My Autobiography*, Kindle locations 463-466.
[74] S. J. Woolf, "Mussolini as Revolutionary," *Journal of Contemporary History* 1, no. 2 (1966): 187-96, http://www.jstor.org/stable/259930.
[75] Mussolini, *My Autobiography*, Kindle locations 708-711.

"hierarchy; the foundation is the Black Shirts and on the summit is the Chief, who is only one," and that one was Mussolini and only Mussolini.[76] His vision of the Fascism was an all-encompassing set of standards for the conduct of each and every person from the inside out, permeating the intellect, the personality, the soul, and even what he poetically described as the "soul of the soul" of the artist, the scientist, the thinker in a "dramatic national self-assertion."[77] Fascism—by design—dominates each and every institution: legal, educational, and even spiritual, not only in form but in content, manifesting in "real conditions of experience."[78] By enforcing discipline with undisputed authority; Mussolini, therefore, chose an emblem to signify justice, unity, and strength: lictor rods, or fasces.[79] A lictor was a Roman official who carried rods, adapted from the Etruscan symbol of penal power, made from gathering sticks together to form a larger staff, onto which the Romans would affix an ax. The ax warned citizens of possible execution as punishment for disobeying the edicts of the Roman magistrates or state. Beginning in 1919, Mussolini's Fascist Party adopted the lictor fasces as their official emblems to be worn as insignia on their uniforms,[80] thus Mussolini intentionally associated himself with the official state power to punish, including with violence, and even to death.

In the United States, the only Western developed country to maintain capital punishment, it is typically the for-profit, private

---

[76] Ibid., Kindle locations 1955-1957.
[77] Martin Gilbert, "The Rise of Fascism in Europe in the Twentieth Century: Lessons for Today," *India International Centre Quarterly* 29, no. 2 (2002): 31-38. http://www.jstor.org/stable/23005773.
[78] Louis Althusser, "Ideology and Ideological State Apparatuses," in *The Critical Tradition*. Edited by David Richter. Boston: Bedford St. Martins, 738.
[79] Mussolini, *The Doctrine of Fascism*.
[80] Peter Struck, "Lictors." *Classics Dictionary*, (University of Pennsylvania, 2000-2009).

power regime that wields the lictors' rods in a simultaneously neoliberal and neoconservative totalitarian scheme that is largely anonymous or "inverted," but that nonetheless has brought about a "demobilization of the citizenry"[81] not by a charismatic leader but by a faceless, nameless corporate "rule of nobody," as Hanah Arendt described it in her seminal text on the continued banality of evil.[82] While some claim that the recent increase in American Corporate-Fascism is the natural response to the terrorist attacks in 2001, as Robert Kagan realizes, "America did not change on September 11, it only became more itself," and it is "an objective fact that Americans have been expanding their power and influence in ever-widening arcs since even before they founded their own independent nation."[83] Most of the signatories to the Declaration were wealthy, all were white males. The majority of both Democrats and Republicans consciously or instinctively condone or promote the new American Corporate-Fascist structure of power. The power of the American Corporate-Fascist brand of totalitarianism is neoliberal because it "seeks to bring all human action into the domain of the market,"[84] and it is neoconservative because it embraces preemptive war,[85] full spectrum military dominance,[86] and total information awareness,[87]

---

[81] Sheldon S. Wolin, *Democracy Incorporated: Managed Democracy and the Specter of Inverted Totalitarianism,* (Princeton, NJ: Princeton University Press, 2010), xviii.

[82] Hanah Arendt, *Eichmann in Jerusalem: A Report on the Banality of Evil* (New York: Penguin, 2006), 289.

[83] Robert Kagan quoted in Andrew J. Bacevich, *The New American Militarism: How Americans Are Seduced by War,* (Oxford: Oxford University Press, Kindle Edition, 2005), p. 13.

[84] David Harvey, *A Brief History of Neoliberalism* (Oxford: Oxford University Press, 2007), 3.

[85] Matthew Raphael Johnson "Can We Get the Truth About a Possible North Korea Showdown?" *American Free Press*, 20 April 2017.

[86] J.P. Sottile, "The Neocon Project for a New Democratic Party," *Buzzflash*, 8 August 2016.

[87] Clyde Wayne Crews Jr. "The Pentagon's Total Information Awareness

all in the service of private property rights in what is ironically referred to as "free" markets that the Pentagon enforces with permanent war.[88]

General George Washington followed Sun Tzu's lessons of ruthlessness in battle, and once Washington became president, he expressed similar undemocratic and elitist sentiments as Socrates does in Plato's *Republic*. Washington lamented to his former aide de camp David Humphreys that in a democracy "the people must feel before they will see or act."[89] After Aristotle,[90] and as the wealthiest of the founders, Washington also fiercely guarded private property rights.[91] Coincidentally, Adam Smith published his landmark *Wealth of Nations* treatise in 1776, and though there is no indication that Washington ever read Smith's work, Washington's own writings, especially his letters, regularly refer to free market dynamics and what prices he might pay or fetch, such as in this 1757 business letter to a trading partner: "These are Articles Sir, I greatly wanted, and must now be oblig'd to buy in the Country…at exorbitant prices…your best endeavours in the Sales will be exerted I hope in my favour" and "sent by my acquaintances to the London Market commands great prices…."[92] It is interesting to read Smith today, though, especially in full context and noting that his now immortal "invisible hand" phrase

---

Project: Americans Under the Microscope?" *Cato Institute*, 26 November 2002.

[88] F. William Engdahl, *Full Spectrum Dominance* (Wiesbaden: Edition Engdahl, Kindle Edition, 2009), 175.

[89] Jeffry H. Morrison, *The Political Philosophy of George Washington*, (Baltimore: John Hopkins University Press, 2009), p. 66.

[90] Lenn Evan Goodman and Robert B. Talisse, *Aristotle's Politics Today*, (New York: SUNY Press, 2008), 22.

[91] Benson John Lossing, *Mary and Martha, the Mother and the Wife of George Washington*, (New York: Harper and Brothers, 1886), 45.

[92] George Washington, The Writings of George Washington from the Original Manuscript Sources, 1745-1799, Volume 2, (Washington D.C.: U.S. Government Printing Office, 1799), 160.

appears only once, barely noticeable in this inauspicious paragraph on page 168 of 348:

> But the annual revenue of every society is always precisely equal to the exchangeable value of the whole annual produce of its industry, or rather is precisely the same thing with that exchangeable value. As every individual, therefore, endeavours as much as he can, both to employ his capital in the support of domestic industry, and so to direct that industry that its produce maybe of the greatest value; every individual necessarily labours to render the annual revenue of the society as great as he can. He generally, indeed, neither intends to promote the public interest, nor knows how much he is promoting it. By preferring the support of domestic to that of foreign industry, he intends only his own security; and by directing that industry in such a manner as its produce may be of the greatest value, he intends only his own gain; and he is in this, as in many other cases, led by an invisible hand to promote an end which was no part of his intention. Nor is it always the worse for the society that it was no part of it. By pursuing his own interest, he frequently promotes that of the society more effectually than when he really intends to promote it.[93]

Smith argues that the invisible hand, in this case, works "to support domestic industry," not transnational corporate finance capital. One wonders what Smith himself would say to the neoliberals who ignore the hundreds of other pages surrounding this invisible hand phrase that Smith may have forgotten by the time he began his next paragraph. The reduction of Smith's philosophy on political economy to a misrepresentative bumper sticker about an invisible hand demonstrates the propagandistic nature of history and philosophy education in the United States

---

[93] Adam Smith, *An Inquiry into the Nature and Causes of the Wealth of Nations*, (University of Chicago Press, Kindle Edition, 2012), 168.

and its service to maintain the wealth and status of the fascistic powers that be. Smith, a professor of philosophy, did however repeatedly discuss the frequent idolization of money and mistreatment of the poor by capitalism at the dawn of the industrial revolution. Here are a few representative examples:

> The inhabitants of a large village, it has sometimes been observed, after having made considerable progress in manufactures, have become idle and poor, in consequence of a great lord's having taken up his residence in their neighbourhood.[94]

> This would generally be inconvenient to the rich, and much more so to the poor. If a poor workman was obliged to purchase a month's or six months' provisions at a time....[95]

> That wealth consists in money, or in gold and silver, is a popular notion which naturally arises from the double function of money, as the instrument of commerce, and as the measure of value....The great affair, we always find, is to get money....In consequence of its being the measure of value, we estimate that of all other commodities by the quantity of money which they will exchange for....To grow rich is to get money; and wealth and money, in short, are, in common language, considered as in every respect synonymous.[96]

> Soldiers and seamen, indeed, when discharged from the king's service, are at liberty to exercise any trade within any town or place of Great Britain or Ireland. Let the same natural liberty of exercising what species of industry they please, be restored to all his Majesty's subjects...that is, break down the exclusive privileges of corporations, and repeal the statute of apprenticeship, both which are really encroachments upon

---

[94] Ibid., 125.
[95] Ibid., 134.
[96] Ibid., 158.

natural Liberty, and add to those the repeal of the law of settlements, so that a poor workman, when thrown out of employment…may seek for it in another trade or in another place, without the fear either of a prosecution or of a removal….Our manufacturers have no doubt great merit with their country, but they cannot have more than those who defend it with their blood, nor deserve to be treated with more delicacy.[97]

Smith also supports progressive real estate taxation, which almost all Republicans and many Democrats today decry as an un-American transfer of wealth:

The necessaries of life occasion the great expense of the poor. They find it difficult to get food, and the greater part of their little revenue is spent in getting it. The luxuries and vanities of life occasion the principal expense of the rich; and a magnificent house embellishes and sets off to the best advantage all the other luxuries and vanities which they possess. A tax upon house-rents, therefore, would in general fall heaviest upon the rich; and in this sort of inequality there would not, perhaps, be any thing very unreasonable. It is not very unreasonable that the rich should contribute to the public expense, not only in proportion to their revenue, but something more than in that proportion.[98]

The current authorities have strayed so far from their supposed intellectual father Adam Smith that many real-estate developers such as Jared Kushner and Donald Trump pay an average one percent in taxes on their income, according to analysis by New York University Professor Aswath Damodaran.[99]

---

[97] Ibid., 174-175.
[98] Ibid., 324.
[99] Max Ehrenfreund, "How Donald Trump and Other Real-estate Developers Pay Almost Nothing in Taxes," *Washington Post*, 4 October 2016.

And even Ronald Reagan's own favorite 20th century Smith protégé, F. A. Hayek, argues against the notion of an infallible free market, for the social welfare state, and for the establishment of a guaranteed universal basic income:

> There is no reason why in a free society government should not assure to all, protection against severe deprivation in the form of an assured minimum income, or a floor below which nobody need descend. To enter into such an insurance against extreme misfortune may well be in the interest of all; or it may be felt to be a clear moral duty of all to assist, within the organised community, those who cannot help themselves. So long as such a uniform minimum income is provided outside the market to all those who, for any reason, are unable to earn in the market an adequate maintenance, this need not lead to a restriction of freedom, or conflict with the Rule of Law.[100]

But the Neoliberals and the Neoconservatives reduce Hayek to a line about the state withdrawing to a "minimal citadel,"[101] which they interpret to suggest that socialism itself is evil and the only solution is unfettered capitalism.[102] U. S. neoliberal and fascistic philosophy holds that legislation is a commodity sold in a free market to the highest bidder, and since the wealthy can buy legislators, they can buy legislation—legislation that benefits the wealthy. It is not an accident that the leading brokers of American Corporate-Fascist legislation calls itself an "exchange" and boast in their online mission statement that:

---

[100] F. A. Hayek, *Law, Legislation and Liberty*, Volume 2, (Chicago: University of Chicago Press, 1982), 87.

[101] Robert M. Solow, "Hayek, Friedman, and the Illusions of Conservative Economics," *New Republic*, 15 November 2012.

[102] Nicholas Wapshott, *Keynes Hayek: The Clash that Defined Modern Economics*, (New York: W. W. Norton & Company, 2011).

The American Legislative Exchange Council is America's largest nonpartisan, voluntary membership organization of state legislators dedicated to the principles of limited government, free markets and federalism. Comprised of nearly one-quarter of the country's state legislators and stakeholders from across the policy spectrum, ALEC members represent more than 60 million Americans and provide jobs to more than 30 million people in the United States.[103]

American Corporate-Fascism, therefore, masquerades as nonpartisan and even egalitarian: anyone can choose to earn billions and spend their billions however they choose, including buying the right not to pay taxes: "We don't pay taxes. Only the little people pay taxes," as billionaire slum-lady Leona Helmsley explained.[104] Those on the left who talk of social programs do so at the risk of tarnishing their reputations as socialists or communists—enemies of the state since the Cold War.[105] Meanwhile, laissez-faire economic theory has devolved into an attitude that we should reduce government regulatory agencies to such diminutive and impotent size that we could strangle them to death, as Grover Norquist urges, in his social movement for the one percent.[106] The movement is largely anonymous and secretive, though, in its quest to relieve the super wealthy of any obligation to pay taxes, which they manipulate Congress to shift to the middle class.[107]

---

[103] Jane Cassidy, "Lobby Watch: American Legislative Exchange Council," *BMJ: British Medical Journal* 343, no. 7830 (2011): 934,

[104] Alexia Fernández Campbell, "How Rich Do You Have to Be to Not Pay Taxes?" *The Atlantic*, 4 October 2016.

[105] Alex Goodall, "Diverging Paths: Nazism, the National Civic Federation, and American Anticommunism, 1933-9," *Journal of Contemporary History* 44, no. 1 (2009): 49-69, http://www.jstor.org/stable/40543073.

[106] Isaac Martin, "A Social Movement for the One Percent," *Berkeley Journal of Sociology* 56 (2012): 4-18, http://www.jstor.org/stable/23345256.

So Smith was prescient: "It is the industry which is carried on for the benefit of the rich and the powerful, that is principally encouraged by our mercantile system," and that which "is carried on for the benefit of the poor and the indigent is too often either neglected or oppressed."[108] Largely by means of propaganda do the powers that be manufacture consent, as Noam Chomsky describes it, for their program that benefits almost exclusively themselves.[109] Edward Bernays penned an early blueprint in 1928 for the public relations campaign that continues through 2017 by the self-styled elites who claim to

> govern us by their qualities of natural leadership, their ability to supply needed ideas and by their key position in the social structure. Whatever attitude one chooses toward this condition, it remains a fact that in almost every act of our daily lives, whether in the sphere of politics or business, in our social conduct or our ethical thinking, we are dominated by the relatively small number of persons— a trifling fraction of our hundred and twenty million— who understand the mental processes and social patterns of the masses. It is they who pull the wires which control the public mind, who harness old social forces and contrive new ways to bind and guide the world.[110]

This is the American Corporate-Fascist philosophy, a selfish Ayn Rand vision where elites direct military and police to maintain power and order in a "morality ends where the gun begins"; what could be more authoritarian?

---

[107] David Cay Johnston, "Trumponomics, Taxes, and the American Worker," *Washington Spectator*, 2 November 2016.

[108] Adam Smith, *Wealth of Nations*, 245.

[109] Noam Chomsky, *Manufacturing Consent: The Political Economy of the Mass Media*, (New York: Pantheon, 2011).

[110] Edward Bernays, *Propaganda*, (New York: Ig Publishing. Kindle Edition, 2004), 37-38.

What are the alternatives? All humans have capacities for competition and cooperation; kindness and cruelty; selfishness and generosity. Distinguished Professor of Anthropology and Geography at the Graduate Center of the City University of New York David Harvey suggests the Zapatista Rebellion in Chiapas, Mexico as one example: "the rebellion…did not seek to take over state power or accomplish a political revolution; it sought instead a more inclusionary politics" by a philosophy of engaging "the whole of civil society in a more open and fluid search for alternatives that would look to the specific needs of the different social groups and allow them to improve their lot."[111] Peace activists Media Benjamin and CODEPINK employ creative demonstrations and civil disobedience direct action in a philosophy that emphasizes "taking action where it truly matters…community grassroots democracy to where the power players are making (awful) decisions and make them listen."[112] And some attempt to dismantle or tame the capitalism that fuels Fascism by reducing their own individual consumption, such as Joshua Fields Millburn and Ryan Nicodemus with their 21st century philosophy of minimalism: "Minimalism is a tool that can assist you in finding freedom…from fear…from worry…from overwhelm…from guilt," and most of all, "Freedom from the trappings of the consumer culture we've built our lives around. Real freedom."[113] Novelist and journalist Arundhati Roy offered this advice at the World Social Forum in 2003: "Our strategy should be not only to confront empire, but to lay siege to it. To deprive it of oxygen. To shame it. To mock it.

---

[111] David Harvey, *A Brief History of Neoliberalism,* (Oxford: Oxford University Press, 2005), 199.

[112] Issues and Campaigns, CODEPINK, accessed 15 July 2017.

[113] Joshua Fields Millburn and Ryan Nicodemus, "What is Minimalism?," The Minimalists, accessed 15 July 2017, http://www.theminimalists.com/minimalism/.

With our art, our music, our literature, our stubbornness, our joy, our brilliance, our sheer relentlessness" and with our "ability to tell our own stories. Stories that are different from the ones we're being brainwashed to believe." She predicts that the "corporate revolution will collapse if we refuse to buy what they are selling -- their ideas, their version of history, their wars, their weapons, their notion of inevitability," pointing to the stark fact that "We be many and they be few. They need us more than we need them, and concluding poetically: "Another world is not only possible, she is on her way. On a quiet day, I can hear her breathing."[114]

---

[114] Arundhati Roy, "Confronting Empire," World Social Forum, 2003, Rat Haus Reality, https://ratical.org/ratville/CAH/AR012703.html.

Finance

"Though this be madness, yet there is method in it."
    —Shakespeare

"The exigencies of such artificial finance hastened the ruin."
    —Benito Mussolini

"We must ask ourselves whether the financial and political power of our largest financial firms poses a threat to the administration of justice."
    —Brooksley Born

Mussolini determined early in his administration that the responsibility of rebuilding the Italian state and leading the people "out of chaos" would require a "proper use and easy flow of capital" through the development of the finance structure.[115] He recalled the fall of Banca Italiana di Sconto and the struggles of banking and industrialist factions as cynicism grew in the suffering middle class. His solution was a comprehensive plan to strengthen capitalism to withstand the pressures and tests of the turbulence of the 1920s and beyond, and he continually negotiated with England, Belgium, the United States and Germany to stabilize Italian currency.[116] He also needed financing to colonize Somaliland, Libya, and Ethiopia, which did not end well; Washington and London were watching, and he wanted to show the world that Italy's banking, commercial, and industrial sectors were now healthy and based on sound financial

---

[115] Mussolini. *My Autobiography*, Kindle locations 1377-1382.
[116] Sally Marks, "Mussolini and the Ruhr Crisis," *The International History Review* 8, no. 1 (1986): 58. http://www.jstor.org/stable/40105563.

policy of his government. He hoped to revalue and stabilize the lira on global currency markets so as to improve Italy's credit worthiness, thus lowering interest rates for Italian debt. His methods were as authoritarian and capitalist as ever, encouraging Black Shirts to move against workers to quash labor demonstrations, preempt strikes on the one hand, and rewarding the wealthy by opposing inheritance tax on the other hand.[117]

Leon Trotsky observed that during interwar Italy, finance capital first neglected the middle and working classes down into despair and once the traditional and normal police and military forces could no longer maintain order among the factions and classes fighting to maintain whatever status they had enjoyed, or merely survive, the more extreme or drastic Fascist measures of Mussolini emerged to create order at the cost of freedom. Once the Fascists ascended to power, they immediately colluded with finance capital to dominate or outright seize control of all organs of the state or civil society, from the executive, the judicial, the military, the police, the schools, and even the press and labor unions—who should logically oppose the dangerous alliance of big business and big government. Trotsky further noted with alarm that Fascist projects in general would not only transfer wealth and power to elites, but would necessarily seek to weaken, if not crush, workers' organizations so as to prevent them from coalescing into an independent proletariat force or movement.[118]

Finance and banking services in the United States have nearly tripled as a percentage of gross national product since 1950,[119] and there is no "business" that bankers find more profitable than war.[120] Regardless of who occupies the White House, Wall

---

[117] Ibid. Kindle locations 2373-2439.
[118] Leon Trotsky, *Fascism: What It Is and How to Fight It.* (Berlin: Barvas Books), Kindle locations 112-124.
[119] Robin Greenwood and David Scharfstein, "The Growth of Finance," *Journal of Economic Perspectives* 27, Number 2, Spring 2013, 3–28.

Street persistently pursues war and military spending as dependable corporate welfare that redistributes wealth from working and middle class taxpayers up to billionaires, corporations, and banks that regularly manipulate Congress to exempt the rich from paying taxes—as Mussolini had.

In the final year of the presidency of William Jefferson Clinton, U.S. and NATO dropped over 20,000 tons of bombs over the now extinct Yugoslavia, including television stations, schools, public housing, waterworks, farmlands, and hospitals[121] in what General Wesley Clark described as a plan to "demolish, destroy, devastate, degrade, and ultimately eliminate the essential infrastructure"[122] of the former Yugoslavia. The Geneva Convention Additional Protocol One specifically outlaws attacks on hospitals as war crimes. But what were the national security interests of the United States in a country on a distant continent? Neoliberal champion President Clinton wanted a war to distract the media from his perjury scandal related to Monica Lewinsky, and he chose the fight with a "communist dictator," as Clinton described Milosevic to Russian President Boris Yeltsin, in order to privatize as much of the Yugoslav economy as possible, especially the finance sector that Clinton's Wall Street paymasters coveted.[123] Yeltsin asked Clinton in a 23 March 1999 letter "On what basis does NATO take it upon itself to decide the fates of peoples in sovereign states?" and warned that military action not sanctioned by the United Nations Security Council could lead to "large scale war."[124] Although Russia did not enter

---

[120] "Bush Bank Tied to Nazi Funding," *The Washington Times*, 17 October 2003.

[121] "Nato Bomb Hits Hospital: Parts of the Hospital Were Reduced to Rubble." *BBC News,* 20 May 1999.

[122] Carl Boggs, *Masters of War: Militarism and Blowback in the Era of American Empire*, (London: Routledge, 2013).

[123] Ed Griffith, "When Clinton Lied, Yugoslavia Died," *New Progressive Alliance*, 11 July 2015.

the hostilities directly, the war was large scale, for the peoples of Yugoslavia. NATO aggression destroyed 14 airports, 19 hospitals, 69 schools, 300 miles of roads, 400 miles of rail, injured over 12,000, killed between 5,000 and 18,000, and contaminated the area with carcinogenic spent uranium munitions[125] that the Joint Chiefs of Staff warned soldiers and civilians not to touch.[126] In contrast, the Saudi-financed attacks of September 2001 on the World Trade Center and Pentagon that justified the never-ending War on Terror claimed only 3 buildings and fewer than 3,000 lives.[127] Years after the NATO bombings, Clinton administration architects of the war John Norris and Strobe Talbott acknowledged that the actual *casus belli* was that Yugoslavia stubbornly maintained a level of socialism that Washington and Wall Street found to be an unacceptable obstruction to their globalist neoliberal privatization plans.[128] As planned, the "reconstruction of the Balkans is exclusively in the hands of Western corporations"[129] today, and British Petroleum recently announced that the Southern Gas Corridor project was right on schedule to deliver 10 billion cubic meters of liquefied natural gas from the Caspian Sea region to European markets by 2020.[130] And in the former Yugoslavian region of Montenegro,

---

[124] John Norris, *Collision Course: NATO, Russia, and Kosovo,* (Santa Barbara: Praeger, 2005).

[125] "US, NATO Lie to Justify Genocide and Destruction in Yugoslavia," *Telesur*, 23 March 2016.

[126] Marlise Simons, "1999 U.S. Document Warned of Depleted Uranium in Kosovo," *New York Times*, 9 January 2001.

[127] Melanie Eversley, "1,113 families still have no real confirmation of 9/11 deaths," *USA Today*, 11 September 2016.

[128] Noam Chomsky, "On the NATO Bombing of Yugoslavia," *Chomsky.Info*, 25 April 2006.

[129] Claudia Von Werlhof, "Neoliberal Globalization: Is There an Alternative to Plundering the Earth?" in *The Global Economic Crisis: The Great Depression of the XXI Century*. Edited by Michel Chossudovsky and Andrew Gavin Marshall, Toronto: Global Research, 2010.

[130] Georgi Gotev, "Southern Gas Corridor on Time, BP executive says,"

neoliberal militarist forces ignored public opinion and relations with Russia and pushed the small country into membership with NATO in early 2017.[131]

While many found Barak Obama charming, elegant, and articulate, voting for him in expectation of extremely vague promises of "change" and "hope," many lost interest after the election. Once in office, Obama proved a good investment for business, though, surrounding himself with Wall Street hawks[132] from "giant vampire squid"[133] banks—just as Bill Clinton had,[134] and Hillary Clinton would have.[135] Much to the pleasure of the Pentagon, Obama quickly became what one veteran journalist described as "a murderer and a terrorist, because the US has a machine that spans the globe, that has the capacity to kill, and Obama has kept it set on kill." Indeed, "Obama seems to have killed more civilians during his first year than Bush did in his first year, and maybe even than Bush killed in his final year," all in the service of the American Corporate-Fascist capitalist state.[136] "This is an old story within capitalist countries, but in the context of a globalized capitalism," engineered by integrated global finance, "it is this logic which increasingly determines just how limited is the room for progressive reform within them," and not simply "because of the strength of external and internal private

---

EURACTIV, 12 May 2016.

[131] Dusica Tomovic, "Russia, Montenegro Trade Barbs Over NATO Membership," *Balkan Insight*, 21 April 2017.

[132] David Dayen, "The Most Important WikiLeaks Revelation Isn't About Hillary Clinton," *New Republic*, 14 October 2016.

[133] Matt Taibbi, "The Great American Bubble Machine," *Rolling Stone*, 5 April 2010.

[134] Shawn Helton, "Partners in Crime: Goldman Sachs, The Clintons and Wall Street." *Global Research*, 3 November 2016.

[135] Robert Yoon, "$153 Million in Bill and Hillary Clinton Speaking Fees, Documented," *CNN Politics*, 6 February 2016.

[136] Allan Nairn, "Obama Has Kept the Machine Set on Kill," *Democracy Now*, 6 January 2010.

capitalist forces that are opposed to progressive reform," but also because of the government institutions themselves depend on the very same private capital finance in order to operate.[137]

President Trump, too, immediately turned to the same Goldman Sachs bankers he had taunted from the campaign trail,[138] promising to reinstate the New Deal Glass-Steagall Act that stabilized banking for decades.[139] The bankers hadn't seen it that way, though, because more regulation meant less leverage and speculation that allowed for more and higher fees and profits.[140] Unfortunately, Trump has forgotten about the bank regulation now that he is in office, and White House Budget Director Mick Mulvaney celebrated a 1 May 2017 fascistic spending bill that found money for 40 miles of border wall fencing and increased military spending, without a similar increase for social programs. In words that could have come from Mussolini himself, Paul Ryan proclaimed: "No longer are the needs of our military going to be held hostage to domestic spending," and President Trump bragged that "This is what winning looks like."[141] Mulvaney announced early in July of 2017 that the Trump Administration would support "broader efforts to streamline government," in part by "reducing the Federal civilian workforce."[142] Mulvaney's

---

[137] Leo Panitch, & Sam Gindin, "Political Economy and Political Power: The American State and Finance in the Neoliberal Era, *Government and Opposition*, 49, 3 (2014): 369-399, doi:http://dx.doi.org.jpllnet.sfsu.edu/10.1017/gov.2014.4.
[138] Matt Egan, "Trump hires yet another Goldman Sachs banker." CNN Money, 16 March 2016.
[139] Thomas MacMillan, "Who Is Gary Cohn? 8 Things You Should Know About the White House Economic Adviser," *Cosmopolitan*, 18 April 2017.
[140] Jon Schwarz, "How Much Does a Politician Cost?" *The Intercept*, 4 May 2017.
[141] S.A. Miller and Stephen Dinan, "'What Winning Looks Like': Trump Gets Border Wall Funds, Money for Military," *Washington Times*, 2 May 2017.
[142] Mick Mulvaney, "Memorandum for the Heads of Departments and Agencies," Office of Management and Budget, 7 July 2017.

plans also project "3 percent economic growth over time," though most economists find the prediction "unrealistic."[143] When the growth does not materialize, we know from examples in Greece, Portugal, and Detroit who will sacrifice and be sacrificed by America's Corporate-Fascists.

Bernie Sanders offers a much different vision of finance and government budgeting. The Sanders inspired Our Revolution website suggests the following alternative solutions:

- *Demand that the wealthy and large corporations pay* their fair share in taxes. Stop corporations from shifting their profits and jobs overseas to avoid paying U.S. income taxes. Create a progressive estate tax on the top 0.3 percent of Americans who inherit more than $3.5 million. Enact a tax on Wall Street speculators who caused millions of Americans to lose their jobs, homes, and life savings.

- *Increase the federal minimum wage* from $7.25 to $15 an hour by 2020. In the year 2015, no one who works 40 hours a week should be living in poverty.

- *Put at least 13 million Americans to work* by investing $1 trillion over five years towards rebuilding our crumbling roads, bridges, railways, airports, public transit systems, ports, dams, wastewater plants, and other infrastructure needs.

- *Reverse trade policies* like NAFTA, CAFTA, and PNTR with China that have driven down wages and caused the loss of millions of jobs. If corporate America wants us to buy their products they need to manufacture those products in this country, not in China or other low-wage countries.

---

[143] Lucy Bayly, "Trump's Budget Assumes 'Unrealistic' Economic Growth, Say Experts," NBC News, 23 May 2017.

- *Create 1 million jobs* for disadvantaged young Americans by investing $5.5 billion in a youth jobs program. Today, the youth unemployment rate is off the charts. We have got to end this tragedy by making sure teenagers and young adults have the jobs they need to move up the economic ladder.

- *Fight for pay equity* by signing the Paycheck Fairness Act into law. It is an outrage that women earn just 78 cents for every dollar a man earns.

- *Make tuition free* at public colleges and universities throughout America. Everyone in this country who studies hard should be able to go to college regardless of income.

- *Expand Social Security* by lifting the cap on taxable income above $250,000. At a time when the senior poverty rate is going up, we have got to make sure that every American can retire with dignity and respect.

- *Guarantee healthcare* as a right of citizenship by enacting a Medicare for all single-payer healthcare system. It's time for the U.S. to join every major industrialized country on earth and provide universal healthcare to all.

- *Require employers to provide* at least 12 weeks of paid family and medical leave; two weeks of paid vacation; and 7 days of paid sick days. Real family values are about making sure that parents have the time they need to bond with their babies and take care of their children and relatives when they get ill.

- *Enact a universal childcare* and prekindergarten program. Every psychologist understands that the most formative years for a human being is from the ages 0-3. We have got to make sure every family in America has the opportunity to send their kids to a high quality childcare and pre-K program.

- *Make it easier for workers to join unions* by fighting for the Employee Free Choice Act. One of the most significant reasons for the 40-year decline in the middle class is that the rights of workers to collectively bargain for better wages and benefits have been severely undermined.

- *Break up huge financial institutions* so that they are no longer too big to fail. Seven years ago, the taxpayers of this country bailed out Wall Street because they were too big to fail. Yet, 3 out of the 4 largest financial institutions are 80 percent bigger today than before we bailed them out. We need to fight to get this legislation signed into law.[144]

Campaigning on a similar platform, Bernie Sanders' 2016 presidential primary success shocked the political establishment and the corporate media that corruptly ignored him.[145] Sanders remains the single most popular politician in the country, according to a March 2017 Fox News Poll.[146] Another promising movement places financing with the people through their local governments in the form of state banks. Commonomics USA and Lieutenant Gavin Newsome have recently touted the advantages of establishing a public bank in California. The state bank would hold tax revenue and could then lend itself, or California residents and businesses, funds that would support local projects and needs without paying transaction fees to unscrupulous Wall Street Banks such as Wells Fargo. The state-owned Bank of North Dakota, for example has funded over $85 million of low-interest public-works projects, farm loans, and student debt.[147] And, as another example of government

---

[144] "Income and Wealth Inequality," Our Revolution, accessed 15 July 2017, https://ourrevolution.com/issues/.

[145] Story Hinckley, "Bernie who? Why does TV Media Ignore Sanders Even as He Tops Polls?," *Christian Science Monitor*, 1 October 2015.

[146] Elizabeth Keatinge, "Fox News Poll: Bernie Sanders Most Popular Politician in America," *USA Today*, 17 March 2017.

outperforming private enterprise, The Bank of North Dakota reported record profits of $136.2 million for 2016, establishing 13 "years of record profits," according to bank president Eric Hardmeyer.[148] At the same time, the 20 largest banks in the world lost over $400 billion in the first two quarters of 2016.[149]

[147] James Rufus Koren, "Should California Start Its Own Bank to Serve Marijuana Companies? It Wouldn't Be Easy," *Los Angeles Times*, 27 July 2017.

[148] Associated Press, "Bank of North Dakota Sees Another Year of Record Profits," *U.S. News & World Reports*, 2 May 2017.

[149] David Reilly, "The Big-Bank Bloodbath: Losses Near Half a Trillion Dollars," *Wall Street Journal*, 6 July 2016.

Labor

"I could hire one half of the working class to kill the other half."
—Jay Gould

"We were directed more and more toward the corporative state."

—Benito Mussolini

"Organized labor is the only way to have fair distribution of wealth."
—Dolores Huerta

Mussolini early in his tenure declared that the Fascist State would abandon the "old system and old ways" of labor unions, so in December of 1923, he explained that: "Peace within is primarily a task of government," and "government has a clear outline of conduct" in which "order must never be troubled for any reason whatsoever."[150] Mussolini would also intimidate or even censor and control Italian papers and film to further his policies.[151] With the Fascists in power, Italy would tolerate no trouble from any quarter, including workers, so "little by little, the old labor structure and associations were abandoned," as the Mussolini administration "directed more and more toward the corporative conception of the state," because the "Fascist State with its corporative conception puts men and their possibilities into productive work and interprets for them the duties they have to fulfill."[152] This is perhaps as stark an admission of

---

[150] Mussolini, *My Autobiography*, Kindle locations 2537-2541.
[151] Marina Nicoli, "Entrepreneurs and the State in the Italian Film Industry, 1919—1935," *The Business History Review* 85, no. 4 (2011): 775-98, http://www.jstor.org/stable/23239424.

totalitarianism as any leader could espouse. Mussolini also condemned labor strikes as acts against the state and the people, therefore acts of treason, as he described in 1920: "The stated cause of the" socialist "agitations was always economic, but in truth the end was wholly political," Mussolini felt, "the real intention was to strike a blow full in the face of the state's authority, against the middle classes and against disciplined order," in a traitorous attempt to establish "the soviets in Italy" by creating "a combination of disorders…in the hands of a tyrannous" socialist minority.[153]

Seven years earlier, in Colorado, the United Mine Workers and their families fought pitched battles with Rockefeller's mercenary strikebreakers from the Baldwin-Felts Detective Agency, who raided the miners' tents with Gatling guns. As the miners resisted and counterattacked, Rockefeller persuaded the governor to call out the National Guard, who beat and arrested the miners, yet the miners refused to return to work or disperse all through the cold winter and into the spring of 1914. At dusk on the 20th of April, the Guardsmen set fire to the miners' tents, sending the women and children fleeing up into the hills, where thirteen died from gunfire. The next day revealed another eleven children and two women dead from fire. When news of what came to be known as the Ludlow Massacre reached Denver, 300 armed strikers gathered to march to the defense of those remaining in the tent colonies. Thousands protested at the Colorado state capital denouncing the governor as an accomplice to murder, and picketers descended on Rockefeller's Broadway office in New York City, but the *New York Times* called for force instead of calm: "With the deadliest weapons of civilization in the hands of savage-minded men, there can be no telling to what

---

[152] Mussolini, *My Autobiography*, Kindle locations 2538-2561.
[153] Ibid., Kindle locations 950-953.

lengths the war in Colorado will go unless it is quelled by force," so the president "should turn his attention from Mexico long enough to take stern measures in Colorado."[154] The Colorado governor requested, and President Wilson sent, federal troops. In the end, over sixty men, women, and children died, but not one guard, militiaman, or federal troop faced a single charge. On the eve of World War I, the United States government clearly established that in clashes between wealthy industrialists and workers, the full and violent force of the state remained at the service of capital against labor.[155]

Decades later, arch conservative presidential candidate and United States Senator from Arizona Barry Goldwater agreed with Mussolini's desire to suppress organized labor, though both men claimed to respect the rights of workers. Goldwater especially bristled at the thought that labor unions might exert political influence, arguing that politics had nothing to do with employment. In his memoir, *Conscience of a Conservative*, Goldwater acknowledges that the industrialization of the nation had attracted workers to cities to work in factories where "wage earners found themselves at a distinct disadvantage in dealing with their employers" due to the vastly superior "economic power of the large enterprises."[156] Goldwater later complains, citing not a single statistic or even incident, that unions leaders had gradually concentrated so much power that they were corrupting politics, encouraging inefficiency, lowering production, and raising prices by forcing contract terms on employers—to the grave danger of the nation itself.

---

[154] Howard Zinn. *A People's History of the United States,* (New York: Harper Collins, 2015), Kindle locations 7721-7773.

[155] Scott Martelle, *Blood Passion: The Ludlow Massacre and Class War in the American West*, (Rutgers University Press, 2008).

[156] Barry M. Goldwater, *Conscience of a Conservative,* (Start Publishing LLC. Kindle Edition), 30-31.

United Nations Special Rapporteur on Freedom of Assembly Maina Kiai found in a 2017 report that although the United States has played an important role in international labor standards and rights, the National Labor Rights Act "legalizes practices that severely infringe workers' rights to associate," and further "provides few incentives for employers to respect workers' rights," especially given the underfunding and weak enforcement of labor law, "compared to the massive resources dedicated to other law enforcement functions in the United States."[157] Corporate forces consistently engineer their own social emancipation of corporate dominance to outweigh social regulation of their activities.[158] As Professor David Harvey describes the current relationship between workers, management, and government: "The state typically produces legislation and regulatory frameworks that advantage corporations," at the expense of workers, and in "many of the instances of public–private partnerships, particularly at the municipal level" of government, the public "assumes much of the risk while the private sector takes most of the profits."[159] When necessary, the American Corporate-Fascist state resorts to "coercive legislation and policing tactics (anti-picketing rules, for example to disperse or repress collective forms of opposition to corporate power," including surveillance, policing, and incarceration as key strategies "to deal with problems arising among discarded workers and marginalized populations," so that the "coercive arm

---

[157] Michelle Chen, "America's Freedom to Protest Is Under Attack," *The Nation*, 6 June 2017.

[158] Boaventura De Sousa Santos, "Beyond Abyssal Thinking: From Global Lines to Ecologies of Knowledges," *Review (Fernand Braudel Center)* 30, no. 1 (2007): 46, http://www.jstor.org/stable/40241677.

[159] David Harvey, *A Brief History of Neoliberalism*, (Oxford: Oxford University Press, 2007), 77.

of the state is augmented to protect corporate interests and, if necessary, to repress dissent" by workers or protestors.[160]

In the 21st century, the government is perhaps more discreet and subtle but no less biased towards corporate interests against the interests of workers than we saw in 1914 Colorado. When legislation and poor enforcement are not sufficient or when workers gather publicly and protest, the Department of Homeland Security and its vast surveillance assets often collaborate with corporate employers to suppress dissent, much in the way the mercenary firm Tiger Swann and the Sheriff's Deputies oppressed and often physically attacked peaceful water protectors and the journalists and celebrities who came to chronicle or join the resistance against the Dakota Access Pipeline: "It's like a Big Brother society, with a private corporation – with even less restraints than the government – totally interfering with our right to privacy, free speech, assembly, and religious freedom," said Jeff Hass of the National Lawyers Guild.[161] The federal government agencies coordinate surveillance assets through what they innocuously refer to as fusion centers,[162] where taxpayers "can count on DHS cadres not to support the Constitutional right of anyone," like pro football player Colin Kaepernick, who refuses to stand during the National Anthem, and similar to the Vietnam War era CIA "Phoenix program it was modeled on, the DHS helps coordinate the systematic corruption and repression of grassroots American society on behalf of the rich corporate elite."[163]

---

[160] David Harvey, *A Brief History of Neoliberalism*, 77.

[161] Antonia Juhasz, "Inside the military tactics used during Standing Rock," *Journal*, 8 June 2017.

[162] Alleen Brown, Will Parrish, and Alice Speri, "Standing Rock Documents Expose Inner Workings of "Surveillance-Industrial Complex," *Intercept*, 3 June 2017.

[163] Douglas Valentine, *The CIA as Organized Crime: How Illegal Operations Corrupt America and the World* (Clarity Press, 2016), Kindle locations 5080-5117.

Three university economists concluded in 2005 that many of the taxpayer funds allocated by Congress to the Department of Homeland Security to protect against terrorism instead buy consent in an ongoing example of colossal pork-barrel waste and utter "government failure."[164]

As an employer, the Department of Homeland Security actively thwarted the rights of its federal workers to civil service and labor union protections, only relenting in February of 2008 after years of battles in courts and the halls of Congress. The fight began at the founding of DHS, when the George W. Bush administration sought "to create a separate personnel system for Homeland Security, changing how employees would be paid, promoted and disciplined," arguing "that the Sept. 11, 2001, terrorist attacks required changes that would give more discretion to managers and permit quicker deployment of workers without notifying their union representatives."[165] The rules proposed through the Office of Personnel Management would have allowed DHS to ignore any contract provision simply by issuing a department directive, but several court decisions rejected the scheme, and Congress ultimately disabled the project by providing no funding whatever for the new human resources management system designed to eviscerate labor rights for workers at DHS.

First Responder grants through DHS amount to as much as $3.4 billion a year in large cities, and monies spent on fighting terrorism in states such as Wyoming, where few likely targets exist but where Congress nonetheless awarded $2 million for "statewide weapons of mass destruction regional emergency response teams."[166] These are monies that are not available to

---

[164] Morris R. Coats, Gökhan Karahan, and Robert D. Tollison, "Terrorism and Pork-Barrel Spending," *Public Choice* 128, no. 1/2 (2006): 275-87.
[165] Stephen Barr, "DHS Withdraws Bid to Curb Union Rights" *Washington Post*, 20 February 2008.

fight more pervasive but equally as pernicious crimes such as human trafficking, especially of children. The United Nations defines the problem:

> Trafficking in persons means the recruitment, transportation, purchase, sale, transfer, harbouring or receipt of persons: by threat or use of violence, abduction, force, fraud, deception or coercion (including the abuse of authority) or debt bondage, for the purpose of placing or holding such person, whether for pay or not, in forced labour of slavery like practices, in a community other than the one in which such person lived at the time of the original act described.[167]

The problem of trafficking for prostitution dates at least back to the nineteenth century with a well-documented migration of women from China to the United States.[168] Prostitution makes money, so a free and unregulated market welcomes the sale of sex. In practice, however, the market is typically dominated by coercion, so it is not free for the person sold, who often cooperates only through force or the threat of force, and corrupt law enforcement officials often condone or perpetuate the coercion,[169] even celebrating it with a recent secret ceremony in Oakland.[170] And while the Central Intelligence Agency estimates

---

[166] Angela Montefinise, "It's a 'Plain' Abusurdity: Wyoming 'Better Funded' Than NYC vs. Al Qaeda," *New York Post*, 8 August 2004.

[167] Annie U. George, U. Vindhya, and Sawmya Ray, "Sex Trafficking and Sex Work: Definitions, Debates and Dynamics — A Review of Literature." *Economic and Political Weekly* 45, no. 17 (2010): 64-73.

[168] Kenneth S. Y. Chew, and John M. Liu, "Hidden in Plain Sight: Global Labor Force Exchange in the Chinese American Population, 1880-1940," *Population and Development Review* 30, no. 1 (2004): 68.

[169] "Two Washington, DC Police Officers Were Previously Arrested for Child Sex Offenses - One for Pimping Out a Missing Girl - in City Shaken by Disappearances of Young Black Girls," *Daily Mail*, 26 March 2017.

[170] Darwin BondGraham and Ali Winston, "Oakland Police Hold Secret

that "there are 50,000 women and children trafficked each year throughout the US for the purposes of commercial sexual exploitation," the Department of Health and Human Services managed to certify only 286 in 2008, "making them eligible for federal and state benefits and services" to create free and productive lives for themselves.[171] Many of those trafficked are born in America and become trafficked in their teens. Attorney General Xavier Becerra announced at a July 2017 news conference that most sex trafficking cases in California involve victims born and raised in the United States: 72 percent of the victims found by authorities in California are American. "Human trafficking, which includes sex and labor trafficking, is one of the fasting growing crimes in the world. Its reach is not limited to foreign countries," said Becerra. "In California, human trafficking is reported here…more than in any other" state.[172] The neoliberal American Corporate-Fascist model encourages business, despises entitlement programs, and ignores corruption, so the trafficking, especially of immigrants continues.

Child labor, too, continues in the United States or for the competitive advantage of U.S. corporations: low wages. A National Labor Committee report uncovered hundreds of children, as young as 11-years-old, sewing clothes for Puma, Hanes, and Wal-Mart, working 12 to 14 hours per day and earning only 6 ½ cents an hour.[173] Charles Kernaghan and the National Labor Committee discovered in 1996 that Kathie Lee

---

Ceremony Honoring Several Officers Accused of Mishandling Celeste Guap Sex-Crimes Investigation," *East Bay Express*, 14 July 2017.
[171] Stephanie Hepburn, and Rita Simon, "Hidden in Plain Sight: Human Trafficking in the United States," *Gender Issues* 27, no. 1/2: 1-26.
[172] Susan Abram, "Massive West Coast sex trafficking ring included 15-year-old sold in 'plain sight.'" *San Jose Mercury News*, 28 July 2017.
[173] Charles Kernaghan, "Child Labor is Back: Children Are Again Sewing Clothing for Major U.S. Companies," National Labor Committee, October 2006.

Gifford's line for Wal-Mart regularly exploited 12 and 13-year-olds in Honduras, and Walt Disney Company similarly employed Haitian children at significantly below the minimum 30 cents per hour rate for their clothing line.[174] Fourteen years later, China Labor Watch revealed that Disney Toys employed 14 to 16-year-old workers at two separate factories, where children worked 12-hour days in "unacceptable conditions," manufacturing Winnie the Pooh and Piglet dolls and stamps, but all Disney corporate officials could offer in response was an evasive platitude: "We have a long-standing commitment to the safety and well-being of our workers. To imply that we do not address that is untrue."[175] The next year, however, Students and Scholars Against Corporate Misbehaviour launched a new investigation of a Disney licensee factory making Cars merchandise after a female employee jumped to her death following a sever public scolding by her managers; the investigation found the following:

- The employment of a 14-year-old. Staff also reported the presence of other child workers, according to the investigator.

- Routine excessive overtime. Employees produced a 'voluntary' document they said they had to sign agreeing to work beyond the maximum overtime legal limit of 36 hours a month, along with wage slips that suggested they were averaging 120 hours of overtime a month.

- A harsh working environment in which workers complained of mistreatment by management. One worker injured on the production line was shouted at and ordered back to work despite needing medical treatment.

---

[174] Deborah L. Spar, "The Spotlight and the Bottom Line: How Multinationals Export Human Rights," *Foreign Affairs* 77, no. 2 (1998): 7.
[175] Martin Hickman, "Disney World in Which Chinese Children 'Toil for 76 Hours a Week,'" *Independent*, 11 November 2010.

- Concerns about the chemicals in use and poor ventilation. Employees claimed three workers had fallen ill. They said they had to hide pots of adhesive and thinners during audits of the factory by its client companies.

- They also claimed that they were paid by the factory to give misleading answers during audits and that they were fined for failing to hit targets. The calculation of wages for different workers was described by Sacom as arbitrary.[176]

Once again Disney turned to obviously meaningless claims and promises: "We take these matters impacting our licensees and business partners very seriously and will continue to evaluate this situation based upon the information available to us."[177] But, an 8-month investigation beginning in July of 2015 found that in eight of Disney factories, workers still faced sham unions, no labor contracts, forced overtime, no compensation for work missed due to work injuries, and child labor. And although Disney instituted an audit regime, when the managers know that "auditors are coming, they make a list to tell us what we should not do or tell, we have to memorize the list and speak accordingly. It is exaggerated lying," according to one worker quoted in the SACOM report.[178] Disney was preparing to open a $5.5 billion amusement park in China and promised that it "would investigate any allegations against its suppliers," again.[179]

---

[176] "Disney Factory Faces Probe into Sweatshop Suicide Claims," *Guardian*, 27 August 2011.

[177] "Disney Probing 'Cars' Toy Factory in China," *Deadline*, 28 August 2011.

[178] Catherine Lai, "Injuries, Long Hours and Low Pay: Disney Failing to Protect Chinese Workers at Supplier Factories Says NGO," *Hong Kong Free Press*, 14 June 2016.

[179] Dion Rabouin, "Labor Groups Criticize Disney Over Worker Conditions at China Suppliers," Reuters, 14 June 2016, http://www.reuters.com/article/us-disney-china-labour-idUSKCN0Z015S.

After child labor human trafficking,[180] one of the most intractable and often hidden workplace oppression issues remains sexual assault and harassment. Between 1993 and 1999 over 36,000 rapes and sexual assaults occurred to workers while on duty, and women are the victims in 80% of the crimes.[181] These numbers, like most statistics about sex crimes, are likely under-reported but still reveal the vulnerability of especially women workers, who fear shame and retaliation for reporting misconduct to employers. Unfortunately, gender stereotyping and patriarchy often exacerbate the mistreatment of women in the workplace, and women with high pay and education or status hardly seem protected, as we have learned from the several overlapping scandals finally coming to light after decades of abuse at Fox News.[182] Abusing power, reminiscent of Jefferson's serial rape of slave Sally Hemmings,[183] executives and celebrities such as Roger Ailes, Bill O'Reilly, and Bill Cosby prey on co-workers or proteges for their own pleasure in exploitation that relies on secrecy and implied or actual retaliation. In a representative exchange between Gretchen Carlson and Roger Ailes, her lawsuit claims that Ailes told her, "I think you and I should have had a sexual relationship a long time ago, and then you'd be good and better and I'd be good and better."[184] Like far too many bosses, Ailes refused to accept that his rejected advances were

---

[180] Department of Labor, "Child Labor, Forced Labor & Human Trafficking," Bureau of International Labor Affairs.

[181] D. T. Duhart quoted in "Sexual Violence & the Workplace," National Sexual Violence Resource Center, 2013.

[182] Harriet Sinclair, "Fox News Sexual Harassment Scandal Grows to Include Political Hopefuls, *Newsweek*, 14 May 2017.

[183] Krissah Thompson, "For decades they hid Jefferson's relationship with her. Now Monticello is making room for Sally Hemings," *Washington Post*, 19 February 2017.

[184] Margaret Talbot, "Fox and Fiends: The End of Roger Ailes," *New Yorker*, 20 January 2016.

inappropriate—and illegal—instead assuming that his job title included perquisites of objectifying any Fox employee. The victims, on the other hand, far too often feel forced to choose between abuse or unemployment.

Increasing labor union membership and participation offer the most effective set of alternatives to labor exploitation, as current public opinion recognizes and supports.[185] The Ministerial Council of the Organization for Economic Development and Cooperation adopted guidelines for Industrial Relations in 1976, including "the right of employees to be represented by trade unions and engage constructive negotiations" with employers.[186] Ralph Nader also recommends demanding that Congress reform key labor legislation:

> In short, Taft-Hartley entrenched significant executive tyranny in the corporate workplace, with ramifications that are more severe today than ever. Union membership is at historic 60-year lows, with only 8 percent of the private economy's workforce unionized. Employer violations of labor rights are routine, and illegal firings of union supporters in labor organizing drives are at epidemic levels.

> Major unions in the United States have rallied around the Employee Free Choice Act, which would begin to repair some of the damage caused by Taft-Hartley and the anti-union culture it engendered. They should also speak out for abolition of Taft-Hartley, and not concede this monumental employer usurpation, during this period of giant multinational corporate power.

---

[185] Costas Panagopoulos and Peter L. Francia, "Trends: Labor Unions in the United States," *The Public Opinion Quarterly* 72, no. 1 (2008): 134.
[186] *Transnational Cooperation Among Labor Unions, Issue 36 of Cornell international industrial and labor relations Reports*, eds. Michael E. Gordon, Lowell Turner, Cornell University Press, 2000), 56.

Once again, neither the AFL-CIO nor other major unions have rallied against what they believe to be the most anti-labor law ever enacted by the federal government. Such chronic resignation would never be the case within the business community were there a similar law on the books stifling their organizational powers for so many years.

It is past time for the repeal of Taft-Hartley. That would be one important step in restoring workers right to organize into unions, achieve a living wage in the Wal-Marts, McDonald's and other workplaces, and in revitalizing American democracy.[187]

It is difficult to see reform without increased union membership, and it is equally difficult to see increased membership without a new legal paradigm for relations between workers and capital. Some commentators such as recommend that union leaders and members must build a movement that includes political action, litigation, administrative advocacy, organizing, protesting, and civil disobedience in an effort to promote worker freedom through solidarity.[188] "Without free, self-respecting, and autonomous citizens there can be no free and independent nations," Vaclav Havel said, and without "internal peace, that is, peace among citizens and between the citizens and the state, there can be no guarantee of external peace."[189]

---

[187] Ralph Nader, "Nader/Gonzalez Demands Repeal of 1947 Taft-Hartley Act Which Stifles Worker Rights Statement," 1 September 2008, Vote Smart.
[188] James Gray Pope, Ed Bruno, Peter Kellman, "The Right to Strike," *Boston Review*, 22 May 2017.
[189] Vaclav Havel. BrainyQuote.com, Xplore Inc, 2017. https://www.brainyquote.com/quotes/quotes/v/vaclavhave152334.html, accessed July 31, 2017.

Family

"Now the next woman I get, I've gotta be the boss."
   —Big Bill Broonzy

"Every man has secrets and shady nooks that are not to be explored."
   —Benito Mussolini

"If you can capture the humanity of a family struggling in an economic crisis, you can make a difference."
   —Emily Blunt

Mussolini traces his name back to a family "prominent in the city of Bologna in the thirteenth century," making the point that in "1270 Giovanni Mussolini was the leader of this warlike, aggressive commune...in the rule of Bologna in the days of armored knights," and feudalism.[190] He describes the Mussolini coat of arms as "a rather pleasing and perhaps magnificent design" with its "six black figures in a yellow field-symbols of valor, courage, force."[191] His autobiography continues narrating his military roots: "Later, in the nineteenth century, the family tie became more clearly defined; my own grandfather was a lieutenant of the National Guard."[192] The *Doctrine of Fascism*, co-written with Giovanni Gentile, explains the Fascist theory of history, in which "man is man only by virtue of the spiritual process to which he contributes as a member of the family, the social group, the nation, and in function of history to which all nations bring their contribution," establishing "the great value of

---

[190] Mussolini, *My Autobiography*, Kindle locations 122-124.
[191] Ibid. Kindle locations 135-136.
[192] Ibid., Kindle location 129.

tradition in records, in language, in customs, in the rules of social life."[193] Again we see in Mussolini's "masterful personality,"[194] a rejection of individualism in that a person is only of importance with respect to the contribution to a unit, even as small as the family. As a husband, Mussolini was consistently unfaithful, regularly betraying his actual wife with a series of mistresses from before the official marriage and all the way through it.[195] His legal wife, Rachelle Mussolini, complained that "three women made me suffer. Against each one of them I fought with all my strength. They were Ida Dalser, Margherita Sarfatti and Clara Petacci," but like a battered spouse, Rachelle blamed "the mistresses, not the husband," for making her as wife "suffer."[196] Mussolini speaks lovingly and respectfully of his wife and daughter in his autobiography: "I was living most modestly with my family" in the 1920s "with my wife Rachele, wise and excellent woman who has followed me with patience and devotion across all the wide vicissitudes of my life," and my "daughter Edda [who] was then the joy of our home. We had nothing to want" and though he saw himself mired in conflict, his family always represented "an oasis of security and refreshing calm."[197] As a father, Mussolini was domineering and controlling, especially of his eldest, Edda, who eventually married a Fascist Party official who was eventually executed by Mussolini for having voted against *Il Duce* in the midst of World War II.[198]

---

[193] Mussolini, *The Doctrine of Fascism*, Kindle locations 83-87.

[194] Giuseppe Flora, "Tagore and Italy: Facing History and Politics," *University of Toronto Quarterly* 77, no. 4: 1025-1057.

[195] Margheritta G. Sarfatti, *The Life of Benito Mussolini*, (Whitefish, Montana: Kessinger Publishing, 2004).

[196] Farrell, *Mussolini*, Kindle locations 1491-1492.

[197] Mussolini, *My Autobiography*, Kindle locations 271-284.

[198] Ibid., Kindle location 12056.

Writing during the American Revolutionary War, Mary Wollstonecraft indicted the oppression of male chauvinism that largely remains today, as evidenced by sexual harassment scandals and the pay gap that stubbornly reminds women that men still exert more power in the economy in a way that often begins and ends in the family. Wollstonecraft presented her first wave feminist critique in response to earlier male writers such as Jean Jacques Rousseau, whom she finds "ingenious" in the clever rhetoric he misuses to "prove" that ideal women should be passive and weak, at least weaker than the men in their environs.[199] She criticizes Rousseau's vision as "brutal" in its subjugation of the wife to a role in the family designed to please her man in "agreeable" manner based on Rousseau's assumption that "man and woman are not, nor ought to be, constituted alike in temperament and character, so it follows of course, that they should not be educated in the same manner," nor should they "be engaged in the same employments."[200] And, even in the 21st century we see prominent echoes of Rousseau's ideal woman, whom he named "Sophy," a woman who is "fond of dress," like Melanja Trump, and who "knows how to dress," like Michelle Obama, because "she has taste enough to dress herself well," like Megan Kelly, though "she hates rich clothes," like Ann Romney, yet "her own are always simple but elegant," like Nicky Haley, and she "does not like showy but becoming things,"[201] like Hillary Clinton, whom the press rarely missed an opportunity to mock for her collection of pantsuits or slight change in hair style,

---

[199] Mary Wollstonecraft, *A Vindication of the Rights of Woman*, (Kindle Edition), locations 1598-1642.

[200] Jean-Jacques Rousseau, *Emilius*, Volume 3 page 176, as cited in Wollstonecraft above.

[201] Jean-Jacques Rousseau, *The Works of Jean-Jacques Rousseau: The Social Contract, Confessions, Emile, and Other Essays*, (Halcyon Press Ltd., Kindle Edition), locations 19398-19399.

while serving as First Lady, Secretary of State, or United States Senator.

President Harding commented on the family and "home making" in his first address to Congress in 1921:

> Home making is one of the greater benefits which government can bestow. Measures are pending embodying this sound policy to which we may well adhere. It is easily possible to make available permanent homes which will provide, in turn, for prosperous American families, without injurious competition with established activities, or imposition on wealth already acquired.[202]

Harding referred here to efforts to reclaim 79,000,000 acres of mostly Southern swamp land that the government sought to convert in order to accommodate increases in population by creating new farm lands, but only without competing with the "established activities" of "wealth already acquired" by those families with superior positions in the social and economic hierarchy. This was a project of friendly evolution of lower families respecting higher families, not an aggressive revolution entirely questioning the role and structure of the family or the individual within the family.

In a reaction to the sexual revolution and the changing family roles with more women going off to work, fundamentalists such as Anita Bryant and Phyllis Schlafly urged a return to traditional family morals, which rejected cohabitation, premarital sex, adultery, recreational drugs, abortion, contraception, and especially homosexuality, but not patriarchy.[203] In a 2006 interview, Schlafly complained that:

---

[202] Warren G. Harding, "First Annual Message," December 6, 1921, Online by Gerhard Peters and John T. Woolley, *The American Presidency Project*.
[203] Robert Whirry. "Understanding Anita Bryant, the Woman Who Declared

The feminist movement has carried on a nasty campaign to make the role of full- time homemaker economically untenable and socially disdained. Feminist books are replete with put-downs of the full-time homemaker, such as Betty Friedan's whining that the suburban housewife lives in 'a comfortable concentration camp' to Ruth Bader Ginsburg's demand that 'all legislation based on the breadwinning-husband, dependent-homemaking-wife pattern' must be eliminated 'to reflect the equality principle.' Many more women have been devastated by the unilateral divorce laws eagerly advocated by feminists than have enjoyed opportunities in the corporate and professional world.[204]

Schlafly's Eagle Forum actively opposed the Equal Rights Amendment movement of the 1970s and remained active up until the 2016 presidential campaign, when internal division over Bryant's support for Donald Trump threatened to splinter the group that had recently warned of the dangers of Sharia law overtaking America.[205]

Professor George Lakoff traces authoritarianism in 21st century politics through to what he calls the "strict father" ethic, expressed by religious conservative figures such as James C. Dobson,[206] who has been "effectively teaching people how to use the strict father model to raise their kids," and promote the "connection between strict father families, right-wing politics, evangelical religion, laissez-faire economics, and

---

War on Gays," *Advocate,* 18 August 2016.

[204] Barbara Ehrenreich and Phyllis Schlafly, "A Dialogue on the Diverging Roles and Responsibilities of the Modern American Woman," *Women's Policy Journal of Harvard* 3, (June 2006): 54.

[205] "Infighting at Eagle Forum over Trump nomination creates uncertainty about group's direction and future." *Southern Poverty Law Center*, 15 April 2016.

[206] Dobson, *The New Dare to Discipline*, (Carol Stream, Illinois: Tyndale Publishers, 1991).

neoconservative foreign policy."[207] Lakoff further describes the "strict father model…with a set of assumptions: The world is a dangerous place, and it always will be, because there is evil out there in the world. The world is also difficult because it is competitive" so there will "always be winners and losers. There is an absolute right and an absolute wrong," and since children "are born bad, in the sense that they just want to do what feels good, not what is right. Therefore, they have to be made good," by a strict father.[208]

A few decades before Lakoff, Walter J. Krueckl offered a more historical and anthropological analysis of the authoritarian nature of family patriarchy in his recently updated monograph *Understanding the Roots of Fascism: A Study of the Sources of Fascism Both Within Ourselves and Society*. Krueckl explains that the patriarchal family requires that "children must prove themselves worthy by being obedient, submissive and 'good' in the authoritarian sense of the word first," and only then will the parent figure show respect and love so that the "premise of the patriarchal family, and thus, the resulting family structure, is strikingly opposed to that of the matriarchal" family tradition.[209] The matriarchal family, in contrast, offers a more nurturing and unconditional love and respect for individual growth on its own terms.[210] Whereas, "the patriarchal family member's growth and development is primarily seen within the narrower context of collective efficiency towards a singular material definition of

---

[207] George Lakoff, *The ALL NEW Don't Think of an Elephant!: Know Your Values and Frame the Debate*, (Claremont, New Hampshire: Chelsea Green Publishing, Kindle Edition, 2014), p. 4.
[208] Ibid.
[209] Walter J. Krueckl, *Understanding the Roots of Fascism: A Study of the Sources of Fascism Both Within Ourselves and Society*, (Vancouver: Grove Street Publishing, Kindle Edition, 2014), 10-12.
[210] Evelyn Reed, *Woman's Evolution from Matriarchal Clan to Patriarchal Family*, (Atlanta: Pathfinder Press, 1975).

successful personal growth" of the individual who "becomes equated with 'production unit' and personal growth and development," toward a mastery "of 'marketable skills' [and] subordinated to the inflated sense of" individual freedom of expression.[211] To mold this traditional type of child, Dobson and others, such as police sergeant Robert Surgenor, recommend spanking, as set forth in the wisdom of biblical verses such as Proverbs 13:24 and King Solomon's advice that the father "that spareth his rod hateth his son."[212] But the research does not bear out the wisdom of Surgenor, Dobson, or Solomon. To the contrary, spanking does not improve child or adolescent behavior, but it does lead to dishonesty, stealing, aggression, depression, anxiety, learning difficulties, as well as a cycle of generational violence: "The more parents spank, the more likely they are to physically abuse their children."[213] Consistent with Mussolini's love of all things war, this traditional and patriarchal American family model creates a war on children and develops children who see violence as normal, necessary, and good.

Family values and family dynamics, however, are modernizing in the United States, and corporal punishment, including spanking, is on the decline. A pediatrician recently published in *Parents* magazine a list of alternatives to spanking:

> 1. *Call time outs.* In a time-out, a child is safely isolated from her family or peers for short periods of time -- generally a minute for each year of age. This gives her time to cool off.

> Example: If your child gets angry with another child, put your child in her playpen or send her to her room. After the time-

[211] Krueckl, *Understanding the Roots of Fascism*, 12.
[212] Robert R. Surgenor, *No Fear: A Police Officer's Perspective*, (Franklin, Tennessee: Providence House Publishers, 1999), 203.
[213] Kelly Wallace, "The Cultural, Regional and Generational Roots of Spanking," CNN, 7 February 2017.

out, you and your child can discuss solutions to the problem that just occurred.

2. *Illustrate the consequences of bad behavior.* The best way to let a child know she's done something wrong is to make the point that undesirable acts can often have undesirable results.

Example: If you can't get your child to clean up her room, remove every toy she's left on the floor until there's precious little left to play with. Just be sure your child is old enough to understand the connection between her action and the punishment.

3. *Treat chronic problems in a variety of ways.* Changing the way you handle a recurring problem can work wonders.[214]

Violence, we know, is self-perpetuating, and with 7 billion persons on the planet, we already have too much violence, we need to remove it from the home and family in order to raise more peaceful children who will then teach peace to the next generation.

---

[214] Loraine M. Stern, "Alternatives to Spanking: A Pediatrician Explains Why Spanking Doesn't Work," *Parents*, accessed 17 July 2017, http://www.parents.com/toddlers-preschoolers/discipline/spanking/alternatives-to-spanking/.

Intelligence

"The enlightened ruler will use only the wisest men to spy."
    —Sun Tzu

"I was always surrounded by spies."
    —Benito Mussolini

"When we make ourselves less free, we're not safer, we're only less free."
    —Molly Ivins

Once in power, Mussolini's Fascists became less overtly forceful and more sophisticated, employing a secret police known as the OVRA, which was so secret that the Fascists never explained the meaning of the acronym of the force that actively discouraged or contained dissent.[215] The OVRA's 700 full-time agents managed an expansive network of informants throughout the country, tapped phones, opened mail, and even logged graffiti in public restrooms, in search of "subversives."[216] OVRA reported over 5000 alleged subversives to the Special Tribunal of the Defense of the State between 1927 and 1929, leading to one death sentence, and hundreds of lengthy prison sentences of 5 to 25 years.[217] And, as is common with most all dictators, Mussolini feared possible contenders and threats to his own power, so he ordered OVRA to spy on all senior Fascist Party officials.[218] Mussolini ignored objections from colleagues Farinacci and

---

[215] Diane Yvonne Ghirardo, "Citta Fascista: Surveillance and Spectacle," *Journal of Contemporary History* 31, no. 2 (1996): 351.
[216] Farrell, *Mussolini*, Kindle locations 5300-5311.
[217] De Felice, quoted in Farrell, *Mussolini*, Kindle locations 5301-5314.
[218] Farrell, *Mussolini*, Kindle location 5315.

Balbo so that "Fascism passed in this way definitively from the disorganized indiscriminate and barbaric violence of the *squadre d'azione* to a rational and systematic system of surveillance and repression."[219] As virtually all sovereign governments throughout history have done, Mussolini's Fascist State also maintained spies on foreign governments, foes and friends alike, often through the diplomatic corps, particularly interested in matters of war and peace, constantly trying to predict which country may or may not fight with or against another country in the coming war.[220]

Nuclear war threats have loomed ominously over the first 200 days of the Trump administration, with threats of confrontation with North Korea, China, and Russia.[221] The threats often begin with clandestine cat-and-mouse intelligence gathering or even sabotage operations conducted by secretive organizations that typically hide or misrepresent their actions from oversight by the voters, the press, and the Congress.[222] Declassified documents reveal several instances during the Cold War in which only the clear thinking of a single individual prevented mutual destruction and global catastrophe.[223] The recklessness of senior United States military and intelligence officials is often staggering to behold.[224] Gary Powers' 1960 May Day U-2 flight over the Soviet Union showed the wanton disregard by the National

---

[219] Montanelli, quoted in Farrell, *Mussolini*.

[220] Ivone Kirkpatrick, *Mussolini: Study of a Demagogue*, (London: Odham Books, 1964), p. 348.

[221] Neil Connor, "China enlists Russia help to avert North Korea crisis," *The Guardian*, 15 April 2017.

[222] Eric Alterman, *When Presidents Lie*, (New York, Penguin, 2005), pp. 19-20.

[223] Alan F. Philips, "20 Mishaps That Might Have Started Accidental Nuclear War," *Nuclear Files*.

[224] Stephen Holmes, *The Matador's Cape: America's Reckless Response to Terror*, (Cambridge: Cambridge University Press, 2007).

Security Administration for both the sovereignty of other countries and the safety of U.S. pilots. Early in Powers' flight plan he crossed into Soviet airspace from Afghanistan, when the Soviet Ministry of Defense began to track the intrusion. Defense Minister Malinovsky informed Communist Party Chairman Khruschev, who ordered antiaircraft units to "shoot down the plane by whatever means," as the Soviets had grown "sick and tired of these unpleasant surprises—sick and tired of being subjected to these indignities."[225] Unknown to Powers at the time, the NSA had recently completed a study concluding that the U.S. should discontinue the overflights: "In view of the improving Soviet air defense effort…the utilization of the aircraft may soon be limited to peripheral operations," in interest of safety.[226] As Powers overflew the Soviet space launching pad at Tyuratam to collect photographic and signal intelligence, the Soviet surface-to-air-missile battalion fired an SA-2 missile that struck his U-2 at over 70,000 feet, damaging the wings and tail but left the cockpit and Powers unscathed. Powers lost control of the plane as the wings broke off, sending the fuselage plummeting and spinning toward earth.[227] Demonstrating remarkable presence of mind Powers climbed out of the cockpit, unfastened his oxygen hoses, and parachuted into custody; the feat was all the more heroic in that the plane was designed to self-destruct in a manner "that it was impossible for the pilot to survive" a collision.[228] Yet, the NSA decided not to inform the pilots of their expendability to the state, similar to Mussolini's

---

[225] James Bamford, *Body of Secrets: Anatomy of the Ultra-Secret National Security Agency.* (New York: Knopf Doubleday, Kindle Edition, 2007), 45-52.
[226] Ibid.
[227] Michael Dobbs, "Gary Powers Kept a Secret Diary with Him After He Was Captured by the Soviets," Smithsonian, 15 October 2015.
[228] Bamford, loc. cit.

attitude that the individual served the state and not the converse. At least Mussolini was honest about his values.

The United States intelligence services, however, have shown not only a proclivity to dishonesty, but often a brazen assumption of impunity—even when committing perjury. Director Richard Helms repeatedly lied to the United States Senate Foreign Relations Committee regarding CIA involvement in the coup that assassinated elected Chilean President Salvador Allende. When prosecuted in 1977, Helms argued that his oath of secrecy permitted him to stonewall or lie to Congress.[229] Fortunately, Judge Barrington D. Parker disagreed, chiding Helms at sentencing: "You now stand before this court in disgrace and shame."[230] The secrecy and dishonesty continued all the way through the Vietnam the presidency of Jimmy Carter, whose national security advisor Zbigniew Brzezinski admitted the falsity of the narrative that the CIA aid to the mujahideen began only after the Soviet army invaded Afghanistan. But the reality, kept secret until recently "is completely different: on 3 July 1979 President Carter signed the first directive for secret aid to the opponents of the pro-Soviet regime in Kabul," and on the same day, Brezinski "wrote a note to the president in which [he] explained that…this aid would lead to a Soviet military intervention."[231] When asked later whether he regretted the provocation, Brzezinski replied: "Regret what? The secret operation was an excellent idea" because we "drew the Russians into the Afghan trap…the day that the Soviets officially crossed the border, I wrote to President Carter, saying, in essence: 'We now have the opportunity of giving to the USSR its Vietnam

---

[229] Thomas Powers, "The Rise and Fall of Richard Helms: Survival and sudden death in the CIA," *Rolling Stone*, 16 December 1976.
[230] Bamford, op. cit., 61.
[231] Chalmers Johnson, *Dismantling the Empire: America's Last Best Hope* (New York: Henry Holt, Kindle Edition, 2010), 11-12.

War.'"[232] And the Helms' mentality has continued; Oliver North of Iran Contra infamy was also working on a "Continuity of Government" plan to suspend the Constitution and intern large numbers of domestic dissidents in case of "widespread internal dissent" or "opposition to a U.S. military invasion abroad."[233] In order to shield their unconstitutional, if not treasonous, actions from oversight by any civil liberty minded officials, Lieutenant Colonel North and his colleagues established exclusive intelligence communication channels through a clandestine network, known as Flashboard, to promote their fascistic agenda in secret.[234]

And the agenda regularly includes operations on and against U.S. citizens. Veteran journalist Gary Webb revealed another scandal related to Reagan's Contras in which gangs of Nicaraguan drug dealers and the CIA sponsored Contras conspired to raise funds by selling crack cocaine in Los Angeles and other U.S. cities. Associated Press journalists Robert Parry and Brian Barger had briefly introduced the story on December 20, 1985 by reporting that three contra related groups had "engaged in cocaine trafficking, in part to help finance their war against Nicaragua."[235] The backlash against those journalists began immediately: "Indeed, the White House waged a concerted behind-the-scenes campaign to besmirch the professionalism of Parry and Barger and to discredit all reporting on the Contras and drugs."[236] But in 1989 came the 1166-page report of the United

---

[232] Ibid.

[233] Peter Dale Scott, "North, Iran-Contra, and the Doomsday Project: The Original Congressional Cover Up of Continuity-of-Government Planning," *Asia-Pacific Journal Volume 9*, Issue 8, Number 1, 21 February 2011.

[234] Bill Moyers, *Secret Government: The Constitution in Crisis*, (Public Affairs Television, 1987).

[235] Office of the Inspector General, "The CIA-Contra-Crack Cocaine Controversy: A Review of the Justice Department's Investigations and Prosecutions," United States Department of Justice.

States Senate Kerry Committee, concluding: "In the name of supporting the Contras," American officials "abandoned the responsibility our government has for protecting our citizens from all threats to their security and well-being."[237] Again consistent with the Helms' approach, CIA Director John Deutch and CIA Inspector General Frederick Hitz categorically denied the allegations: "The agency neither participated in nor condoned drug trafficking by Contra forces."[238] The final official report admitted only indirect involvement: "CIA did make contact with prosecutors in the Zavala prosecution in order to protect what CIA believed was an operational equity, i.e., a Contra support group in which it had an operational interest," and a "CIA cable indicates that approximately $36,000 seized from Zavala at the time of his arrest was returned to Zavala--based on the claim they were Contra funds--by the prosecutors at CIA's request," claiming that "the prosecutors state that the decision to return Zavala's money was based on other considerations," not the CIA's representations, "and that there was no evidentiary value to retaining the money."[239] Lead investigator for the Kerry committee Jack Blum, however, testified that "if you ask whether the United States government ignored the drug problem and subverted law enforcement to prevent embarrassment and to reward our allies in the Contra war, the answer is yes," causing

---

[236] Peter Kornbluh, "Storm over 'Dark Alliance,'" *Columbia Journalism Review*, January/February 1997.

[237] Subcommittee on Terrorism, Narcotics, and International Operations, "Drugs, Law Enforcement and Foreign Policy," (Washington: U.S. Government Printing Office, 1989), United States Senate Report 100-165.

[238] Jennifer Auther, "Deutch Confronts Angry L.A. Residents in Town Hall Meeting," *CNN*, 15 November 1996.

[239] Office of Inspector General Investigations Staff, "Report of Investigation Concerning Allegations of Connections Between CIA and the Contras in Cocaine Trafficking to the United States," Central Intelligence Agency, 29 January 1998.

United States Representative from Los Angeles Maxine Waters to argue that it "doesn't make any difference whether [the CIA] delivered the kilo themselves, or they turned their heads while somebody else delivered it, they are just as guilty."[240] Syndicated columnist Carl T. Rowan editorialized that if "this is true, then millions of black lives have been ruined" and our prisons "are now clogged with young African-Americans because of a cynical plot by a CIA that historically has operated in contempt of the law."[241] In the end, it was only Gary Webb and the drug addicts and street dealers who suffered any consequences. In what was likely motivated largely by jealousy of Webb by journalism colleagues seeing the millions of his newfound readers, the profession collectively ostracized Webb, who eventually committed suicide after years of vilification, unemployment, and depression that currently threaten Edward Snowden and Chelsea Manning.[242]

Yale Professor of History Snyder warns us in his 2017 book on tyranny that during "the campaign of 2016, we took a step toward totalitarianism without even noticing by accepting as normal the violation of electronic privacy," and the "theft, discussion, or publication of personal communications destroys a basic foundation of our rights" because if "we have no control over who reads what and when, we have no ability to act in the present or plan for the future," indeed whoever "can pierce your privacy can humiliate you and disrupt your relationships at will."[243] George Washington University Professor of Law Jonathan Turley

---

[240] Kornbluh, loc. cit.

[241] Ibid.

[242] Alex Hannaford, "The CIA, the Drug Dealers, and the Tragedy of Gary Webb," *Telegraph*, 21 March 2015.

[243] Timothy Snyder, *On Tyranny: Twenty Lessons from the Twentieth Century*, (Crown/Archetype. Kindle Edition, 2017), 88.

recently listed the following ominous offences of the intelligence state and its secret budget:

Assassination of U.S. Citizens: President Obama approved the killing of Anwar al-Awlaqi and another citizen. The Obama Administration, as had the Bush Administration, affirmed their assertion that the president can order the assassination of any person involved with terrorism anywhere.

Indefinite Detention: In a 2012 law, the president can also indefinitely detain any citizen merely by accusing the person of terrorism or connections with terrorists.

Arbitrary Justice: Both Presidents Bush and Obama also decided whether a person would receive a civilian trial in open federal court or in a military tribunal that lacks many basic due process protections.

Warrantless Searches: The president can order warrantless surveillance, though the NSA collects virtually all electronic signals anywhere it can. President Obama expanded the Bush Administration practices to include additional business documents.

Secret Evidence: Federal prosecutors regularly present secret evidence as grounds to detain suspects and even try them in federal and military courts. The federal government also forces the dismissal of embarrassing or inconvenient civil cases simply by filing declarations that allowing a citizen a day in court would force the government to reveal classified information that would harm national security. Certain court legal opinions are even classified, which allows the government to claim secret legal arguments to support secret proceedings using secret evidence.

War Crimes: President Obama announced in 2009 that he would not allow CIA employees to be prosecuted for the waterboarding and other well-document torture programs of the Bush Administration.

Immunity from Judicial Review: The Obama Administration continued the Bush policy and practice of claiming immunity for private companies that assist government surveillance of citizens, even when conducted without warrant. This prevents virtually any independent monitoring of the programs, other than by whistleblowers.

GPS Monitoring of Citizens: The Obama Administration successfully defended its claim that it can monitor every move or targeted citizens without court order or review.

Extraordinary Rendition: When federal authorities want even greater latitude in detaining, interrogating, or torturing suspects, they transfer noncitizens and citizens alike to other countries with brutal and dictatorial regimes and long documented histories of human rights abuses.[244]

And the spying began before the terrorist attacks of 2001 in a program named Echelon, employing listening posts around the world to eavesdrop on suspects. The U.S. National Security Agency, with its counterparts in New Zealand, Britain, Canada, and Australia collected virtually all available electronic communications for analysis by super computers—before 2001. In a 2000 interview with CBS *60 Minutes*, a Canadian intelligence officer expressed his concern that the concern that joint project included "no accountability and nothing, no safety net in place for the innocent people who fall through the cracks." The officer listed examples abuses: a mother was labeled as possible terrorists merely for using the metaphor that her son had

---

[244] Jonathan Turley, "10 reasons the U.S. Is no Longer the Land of the Free," *Washington Post*, 13 January 2012.

"bombed" in a school play; the regular practice of one country spying on the citizens of another country so as to create plausible deniability for each country that is violating its own laws by invading the privacy of citizens or prominent politicians such as Margaret Thatcher, Strom Thurmond; and the use of the system to aid corporations in spying on each other to gain contract bidding and other business advantage.[245]

Yet some see hope for the future. In a recent interview, University of California Professor of History Emerita Angela Davis noted that "there is a popular understanding of the connection between racist police violence and systemic issues. The prison-industrial complex has something to do with the CIA's use of secret prisons and the torture that was recently revealed," which may create "a foundation for a movement…there's a powerful foundation and people are ready for a movement."[246] The foundation calls for an all-encompassing movement, and it must dismantle the intelligence leviathan.

---

[245] Steve Kroft, "Ex-Snoop Confirms Echelon Network," *60 Minutes*, 24 February 2000, http://www.cbsnews.com/news/ex-snoop-confirms-echelon-network/.
[246] Angela Y. Davis, *Freedom Is a Constant Struggle: Ferguson, Palestine, and the Foundations of a Movement,* (Haymarket Books, Kindle Edition, 2016), 36-37.

Economy

"Money to attain power, power to protect money."
    —Medici

"I had to establish severest economy in every branch of state administration."
    —Benito Mussolini

"Economics are the method; the object is to change the heart and soul."
    —Margaret Thatcher

Mussolini began enacting his economic plan by striking what he described as "a smashing blow to useless expenditures, and to those who sought tribute from the treasury" because he "had to rake up tax-slackers" and to "establish severest economy in every branch of state administration" in order to "put a brake on the endless increase of employees" so as to be able to settle "debts to foreign powers."[247] Then, in 1923 he "concluded a series of commercial treaties, with a political background, with a number of nations" in an effort to improve Italy's economic position.[248] He signed the Italian-Swiss treaty, the Washington treaty to limit naval arms, and commercial treaties with Czechoslovakia, Poland, Spain, France, and even Russia. He later wrote in a *Gerarchia* article that while many in the nineteenth century believed that capitalism required democracy, in the twentieth century, Mussolini argued, democracy was not necessary: "Democracy in the factory has lasted only as long as a bad dream," so the Italians would replace it with a more efficient

---

[247] Mussolini, *My Autobiography*, Kindle locations 2393-2396.
[248] Ibid., Kindle Locations 2295-2299.

"Fascist trenchocracy."[249] As early as 1928, Dartmouth College Professor of Political Science William Kilborne Stewart observed that Fascism "seems to be simply a dictatorship of the upper classes...."[250] The *Doctrine of Fascism* explains economics in heroic and spiritual terms: "Fascism believes now and always in sanctity and heroism, that is to say in acts in which no economic motive - remote or immediate - is at work," having "denied historic materialism, which sees in men mere puppets on the surface of history, appearing and disappearing on the crest of the waves while in the depths the real directing forces move and work," but Fascism "denies the immutable and irreparable character of the class struggle which is the natural outcome of this economic conception of history" in which class struggle brings about a general social transformation.[251]

President Warren G. Harding seemed to agree more than disagree with Mussolini about democracy in the factory in Harding's 1921 State of the Union Address to Congress:

> Just as it is not desirable that a corporation shall be allowed to impose undue exactions upon the public, so it is not desirable that a labor organization shall be permitted to exact unfair terms of employment or subject the public to actual distresses in order to enforce its terms....just as we are earnestly seeking for procedures whereby to adjust and settle political differences between nations without resort to war, so we may well look about for means to settle the differences between organized capital and organized labor without resort to those forms of warfare which we recognize under the name of strikes, lockouts, boycotts, and the like.

---

[249] Farrell, *Mussolini*, Kindle locations 3155-3160.
[250] William Kilborne Stewart, "The Mentors of Mussolini," *The American Political Science Review* 22, no. 4 (1928): 843-69. doi:10.2307/1945351.
[251] Mussolini, *Doctrine of Fascism*, Kindle Locations 240-251.

Harding equates strikes and boycotts with war; the Harding administration in practice, like all before and after it, consistently favored the interests of capital and disfavored the interests of labor; President Woodrow Wilson had recently set fascistic precedents by seizing control of the railroads and the telephone systems in the name of national security.[252] Then in 1922, Harding's Attorney General Harry M. Daugherty sent in U.S. Marshalls to break up a railroad strike, accusing the workers of an illegal communist conspiracy, prompting the 11 September 1922 *Chicago Tribune* front page headline to announce: "Daugherty to Stand Pat on His Injunction."[253]

More than a century before Harding and Mussolini, Adam Smith discussed the emerging inequity and exploitation inherent in capitalism at the beginning of the American Revolution, noting that the interests of manufacturers often run in contrast to the interest of the public because the industrialists benefit by stifling competition, creating scarcity, and thereby increasing the expenses for their fellow-citizens for the profit of "an order of men, whose interest is never exactly the same with that of the public"; an order of men "who have generally an interest to deceive and even to oppress the public," and who have "upon many occasions, both deceived and oppressed" the general public.[254] This astute analysis by Smith, which anticipates similar criticisms by Karl Marx decades later, lends a much fuller view of so-called free markets than the reductionism of the bumper-sticker adage of the invisible hand metaphor so often repeated by those who have likely not bothered to read Smith,

---

[252] Matthew C. Waxman, "The Power to Wage War Successfully," *Columbia Law Review* 117, no. 3 (2017): 662, http://www.jstor.org/stable/44177166.
[253] "Daugherty to Stand Pat on His Injunction," *Chicago Tribune*, 11 September 1922.
[254] Adam Smith, *An Inquiry into the Nature and Causes of the Wealth of Nations*, (University of Chicago Press), 98-99.

much less Marx. These business interests continue to manipulate and exploit markets to distort them into entities that are anything but free. Rami Zurayk, professor of agriculture and food sciences at American University of Beirut, noted in a recent *Guardian* article that the near monopoly of international grain markets by Cargill and Archer Daniels Midland caused a 37 percent spike in bread prices in 2008, severely straining family budgets all around the world, while simultaneously increasing corporate profits for wealthy shareholders whose families never worry about missing a meal.[255] This is neoliberal capitalism that is perhaps even less democratic in the 21ˢᵗ century than it was in Mussolini's Fascist Italy.

Thomas Piketty's 2014 polemic *Capital in the Twenty-First Century*, argues that it is time to rethink economics to solve such questions as how to bring capitalism and democracy into harmony. Piketty applies vast data from multiple sets to show that far from producing freedom of opportunity, as Milton Friedman and S. A. Hayek argue, the current design of global capitalism amounts to trickle-up economics, or looting from the top. As one reviewer simplified Piketty's argument, it amounts to "r > g….the rate of return on capital (r) is greater than the overall growth rate of the economy (g)" so that "over the history…financial investments and land — capital — have yielded returns of about four to five percent a year on their base value."[256] Since overall growth in the economy has hovered between one and two percent per year, finance capital has continually accumulated more and more of the overall economy by means of compound interest. At five percent, which sounds modest, wealth doubles every fourteen years, but at two percent

---

[255] Rami Zurayk, "Use Your Loaf: Why Food Prices Were Crucial to the Arab Spring," *The Guardian*, 16 July 2011.

[256] Jedediah Purdy, "To Have and Have Not, *Los Angeles Review of Books*, 24 April, 2014.

wealth doubles after thirty-five years. The implications are many, including the statistic that the top one percent of U.S. households, mainly through investments, own thirty-five percent of wealth, and the top ten percent own over seventy percent.[257] Many of these Americans pay little or no income tax, and few even work. This new Gilded Age has also shrunk the middle class and shifted the tax burden onto them by corrupting every level and arm of government.[258] And when the so called "free market" fails, as it did again in 2007, the investor class knows that they can depend on government to rescue the wealthy at the cost of the workers, who find themselves with less and less return on their tax dollars and paying more and more for such public goods as health care and education.[259]

Many apologists for capitalism, such as the John S. and James L. Knight Professor of Business Journalism at Columbia University Sylvia Nasar, cast entrepreneurs like Ivanka Trump and Jared Kushner, as economic heroes who will, by their "genius" and Schumpeterian "creative destruction" raise living standards for all.[260] Ivanka Trump's genius seems to lie and exploiting her celebrity, but there is no evidence that her entrepreneurship is improving the lives of any workers in factories producing her clothing lines.[261] And Kushner's efforts

---

[257] Jesse Bricker, Alice Henriques, Jacob Krimmel, and John Sabelhaus, "Measuring Income and Wealth at the Top Using Administrative and Survey Data," *Brookings Papers on Economic Activity*, (2016), 261-312.

[258] Peter R. Orszag and William G. Gale, "The Great Tax Shift," Brookings Institute, 4 May 2005, https://www.brookings.edu/articles/the-great-tax-shift/.

[259] Simon Marginson, "Economic and Social Inequality," in *The Dream Is Over: The Crisis of Clark Kerr's California Idea of Higher Education*, 143-51. Oakland, California: University of California Press, 2016.

[260] Sylvia Nasar, "The Grand Pursuit of Alfred Marshall and Joseph Schumpeter: The Firm, the Entrepreneur, and Economic Growth," *Proceedings of the American Philosophical Society* 157, no. 1 (2013), 62.

[261] Krithika Varagur "Revealed: Reality of Life Working in an Ivanka Trump Clothing Factory, *Guardian*, 13 June 2017.

seem to center around manipulating markets and foreign finance sources through attempts to peddle influence, which would not benefit any poor since the poor do not finance billion dollar real estate deals.[262] Nor do innovative companies such as Apple show evidence of raising living standards for their poor workers, who earn as little as $1.50 an hour in Dickensian conditions so that others can enjoy the latest iPhone model.[263] According to a 2016 analysis by the MIT Technology Review: "Today Apple contractors assemble iPhones in seven factories—six in China and one in Brazil," but if the same phones "were assembled in the U.S." the change would add a mere "$30 to $40 to the cost."[264] Apple, like most all ostensibly American corporations, consistently place return to Apple shareholders above wages for Apple workers, and Congress rewards rather than punishes the behavior with billions in corporate welfare tax breaks.[265] The innovative approach to evading corporate taxes is indeed both creative and destructive, as Schumpeter predicted, but since most poor workers do not own Apple stock but do pay taxes from their wages; the neoliberal American Corporate-Fascist economy, therefore, worsens living conditions for most, especially given the skyrocketing costs of health care in the United States and the specter that the GOP will likely only aggravate matters—once again in order to deliver tax breaks to the super wealthy who donate to campaigns. [266] Additionally, the mythology of the

---

[262] Bess Levin, "Is Jared Kushner Punishing Qatar Over a Soured Real-Estate Deal?," *Vanity Fair*, 10 July 2017.

[263] Kevin Smith, "Chinese Workers Making iPhones Work 11-Hour Shifts, 6 Days A Week, For $1.50 Per Hour," *Business Insider*, 29 July 2013.

[264] Konstantin Kakaes, "The All-American iPhone," *MIT Technology Review*, 9 June 2016.

[265] Greg LeRoy, "Tens of Billions in 'Corporate Welfare' Tax Deals about to be Exposed Like Never Before," CNBC, 11 July 2017.

[266] Stephen Ohlemacher, "Senate GOP Health Bill: Tax Cuts for Rich," Fox Business, 22 June 2017.

entrepreneur as savior of the poor makes no sense in the context of the finance sector, where banks and insurance companies create nothing, and innovations in financial engineering consistently devise schemes that only hurt the poor through more and higher fees for services, sometimes charging a staggering 30 percent interest; according to a 2016 report by the California Department of Business, 236 licensed payday lenders underwrote over 11 million loans totaling over $3 billion, earning a staggering $458 million in fees.[267] These finance entrepreneurs as lenders are richer, the poor are poorer.

Many of the most vulnerable victims of neoliberal American Corporate-Fascist economics often vote for politicians who further the austerity model that results from cutting taxes and government services to maximize capital for the wealthy. Thomas Frank discusses this phenomenon well in his bestselling book *What's the Matter with Kansas?: How Conservatives Won the Heart of America.* But, importantly, the race to bottom of slashing of government budgets has recently confronted stark reality in Kansas, where Governor Sam Brownback had pursued trickle-down economics with fervor. Brownback and the Republican-controlled legislature eliminated state income tax for many small business owners and cut most other taxes as well as most government services in what Brownback boasted as "a shot of adrenaline into the heart of the Kansas economy."[268] The growth that Brownback promised never occurred; instead, neighboring states with higher taxes and more government services consistently outperformed Kansas, as even the

---

[267] Chriss W. Street, "Report Reveals California Seniors Biggest Users of Payday Loans," Breitbart, 12 Jul 2017, http://www.breitbart.com/california/2017/07/12/report-reveals-california-seniors-biggest-users-of-payday-loans/.
[268] Eugene Robinson, "Robinson: Kansas Learns Lesson of Trickle-down Experiment," *Washington Post*, 12 June 2017.

conservative *Weekly Standard* recently admitted: "It is true that the cuts haven't been a miracle cure for the Kansas economy," and Kansas "has underperformed on jobs and growth."[269] Kansas funding for public schools under the Brownback austerity plan was so low that the state courts had to intervene: "The Kansas Supreme Court…issued a unanimous decision in *Gannon v. State*, holding that the Kansas K-12 public education financing system does not meet the adequacy requirements of the people's constitution."[270] The true benefactors of neoliberal American Corporate-Fascist economics are the architects of it, not lower or middle class public school students or teachers.

In many U.S. cities, students, teachers, and many other workers experience much difficulty affording housing. California housing markets are particularly overpriced, even after voters approved $5 billion in affordable-housing bonds in 2002 and 2006. The California Department of Housing estimated, however, that the state needed to add 180,000 per year to keep pace with demand over the last decade, well more than the 80,000 that developers actually built. "California is in the most intense housing crisis in our state's history," according to Assemblyman David Chiu, of San Francisco: "For the millions of Californians who are suffering, Sacramento needs to act."[271] Sacramento housing advocate Brian Augusta argues that additional supply will not solve the crisis without "some kind of intervention by the state," because California "housing is going to continue to be out of reach for low-income people who pay upwards of 50, 60, 70 percent of their income on rent."[272]

---

[269] Stephen Moore, "What's the Matter with Kansas Republicans? *Weekly Standard*, 22 May 2017.
[270] Meg Wickham, "KS Supreme Court Finds School Funding Unconstitutional," Kansas Bar Association, 2 March 2017.
[271] Melody Gutierrez, "California housing crisis spurring lawmakers into action," *San Francisco Chronicle*, 14 July 2017.

Neoliberal American Corporate-Fascist policy promises freedom, but little real opportunity, except for the already wealthy and powerful.

As Distinguished Professor of Anthropology and Geography at the Graduate Center of City University of New York David Harvey reminds us, "Gérard Duménil and Dominique Lévy...concluded that neoliberalization was from the very beginning a project to achieve the restoration of class power," by imposing neoliberal policies beginning in the late 1970s so that "the share of national income of the top 1 per cent of income earners in the US soared," reaching 15 percent by the end of the century, and the "top 0.1 percent of income earners in the US increased their share of the national income from 2 per cent in 1978 to over 6 per cent by 1999," while compensation for workers compared "to the salaries of CEOs increased from just over 30 to 1 in 1970 to nearly 500 to 1 by 2000."[273] The billionaires designed American Corporate-Fascist economics to serve billionaires, and the gross economic inequality is entirely acceptable to self-styled conservatives, such as Barry Goldwater, who wrote that the "true Conservative...revolted at the attempt to solve," economic problems "by a mob tyranny that paraded under the banner of egalitarianism."[274] Workers are tyrants and mobsters to Goldwater. More recent so called liberal politicians, however, have furthered the trickle-up cause as much as or more than so called conservatives. While some pundits were attempting to tarnish Barak Obama as a socialist,[275] his

[272] Angela Hart, "'Yes in My Backyard.' Silicon Valley Money Fuels Fight Against State's Housing Crisis, 17 July 2017.
[273] David Harvey, *A Brief History of Neoliberalism*, (Oxford: Oxford University Press, Kindle edition, 2007), 16-17.
[274] Barry M. Goldwater, *Conscience of a Conservative*. (Jersey City: Start Publishing, Kindle Edition, 2013), p 7.
[275] Monica Crowley, "Socialist Red Is the New Black: Obama's Leftist Policies Are Changing the Very Nature of America," *Washington Times*, 24

presidency continued the Wall Street bailout program begun under George W. Bush and prosecuted not a single banker for the massive fraud upon the taxpayers who funded the bailout.[276] The hyperbole was commonplace, though: "Notice that Obama keeps saying that 'the rich,' a crass term implying low class social envy, don't 'need' the Bush tax cuts," so *Forbes* contributor Peter Ferrara went on to warn us: "That is reminiscent of the fundamental Marxist principle, 'From each according to his ability, to each according to his need.'"[277] Harvard University Professor of Divinity Cornel West, however, pointed out the starker reality: "Bernie Sanders gallantly tried to generate a leftwing populism but he was crushed by Clinton and Obama in the unfair Democratic party primaries," so America enters "a neofascist era: a neoliberal economy on steroids, a reactionary repressive attitude toward domestic 'aliens,' a militaristic cabinet eager for war and in denial of global warming," and all while "we are seeing a wholesale eclipse of truth and integrity in the name of the Trump brand, facilitated by the profit-hungry corporate media."[278]

The response, though, has been impressive and may become revolutionary. As veteran media and social critic Michael Parenti notes in *Profit Pathology and Other Indecencies*, the Occupy Wall Street movement caught the establishment by surprise and created political space for Bernie Sanders not only to run as a self-identifying democratic socialist but for Sanders to continue his campaign after the inauguration of Donald Trump and do so in a manner and intensity that many plainly refer to as a

---

June 2015.

[276] "Bush Agrees to Obama Bailout Request," CBS, 9 January 2009.

[277] Peter Ferrara, "Is President Obama Really a Socialist? Let's Analyze Obamanomics," *Forbes*, 20 December 2012.

[278] Cornel West, "Pity the Sad Legacy of Barak Obama," *Guardian*, 9 January 2017.

revolution.[279] Civic participation after the election reflects the revolutionary spirit of citizens who have taken to the streets chanting "What do we want? Trump's tax returns. When do we want it? Now" and "We want a leader, not a tax cheater. We want a leader, not a friggin' tweeter."[280] In South Carolina at a congressional town hall meeting at Aiken Technical College, constituents carried red signs charging "you lie" and shouted the phrase at Republican Joe Wilson because of his claims to defend his effort to repeal and replace the Affordable Care Act.[281] The courts are another site of the rebellion; Trump now faces multiple suits against his profiteering on his presidency,[282] water protectors won a legal victory against the administration's rushed approval of the multi-billion dollar Dakota Access Pipeline,[283] Trump's Muslim travel ban remains the subject of several legal battles in several states and is already in front of a skeptical U.S. Supreme Court,[284] and a project of Trump supporter Kelcy Warren.[285] The Women's March on the day after the inauguration, however, set the new standard for the people's revolution.[286]

---

[279] Jason Le Miere, "Bernie Sanders Still Wants a Revolution," *Newsweek*, 31 March 2017.

[280] John Cassidy, "The Trump Resistance: A Progress Report," *New Yorker*, 17 April 2017.

[281] Phil Helsel, "Rep. Joe Wilson's 'You Lie' Line Used Against Him at Contentious Town Hall," NBC, 11 April 2017.

[282] Julie Bycowicz, "Democrats in Congress File Suit Against Trump for Violating Emoluments Clause," *Christian Science Monitor*, 14 June 2017.

[283] Jake Johnson, "In 'Significant' Win for Water Protectors, Judge Orders Review of DAPL Permits," Common Dreams, 15 June 2917.

[284] Alicia Parlapiano and Anjali Singhvi, "The Supreme Court Partially Allowed Trump's Travel Ban. Who Is Still Barred?," *New York Times*, 19 July 2017.

[285] Kris Maher, "Dakota Pipeline's Builder Says Obstacles Will Disappear Under Donald Trump.
CEO Kelcy Warren 'Pretty Confident' About Completion; Trump Has Investment in Company," *Wall Street Journal*, 16 November 2016.

---

[286] Heidi M. Przybyla and Fredreka Schouten "At 2.6 Million Strong, Women's Marches Crush Expectations," *USA TODAY*, 21 January 2017.

Society

"Where justice is denied...society is an organized conspiracy."
   —Frederick Douglass

"I have never flattered the crowd, nor wheedled any one."
   —Benito Mussolini

"A rat in a maze is free to go anywhere, as long as it stays inside the maze."
   —Margaret Atwood

Partly inspired by Mussolini and his Fascists, Italian authorities issued over 600,000 rifle permits and 200,000 pistol permits in the month of December 1921 alone.[287] But Mussolini believed that class war could not transform Italian society, rejecting socialism as "nothing...but the sentimental aspiration—as old as humanity itself—towards a social convention in which the sorrows and sufferings of the humblest shall be alleviated."[288] And he rejected democracy because he could not accept that "the majority, by the simple fact that it is a majority, can direct human society; it denies that numbers alone can govern by means of a periodical consultation," in a democratic system that "may be defined as from time to time giving the people the illusion of sovereignty, while the real effective sovereignty lies in the hands of other concealed and irresponsible forces," in society.[289] He explained that "the Fascist conception of authority has nothing" in common with a "feudal system...and the division of society into castes."[290] In practice, however, Fascist governance sought

---

[287] Farrell, *Mussolini*, Kindle locations 3142-3144.
[288] Mussolini, *My Autobiography*, Kindle locations 2882-2885.
[289] Ibid., Kindle locations 2888-2891.

to create a society in which the individual sacrificed material well-being and even most democratic and civil rights in the service of the Fascist State, a warring and expanding state.[291] President Eisenhower's farewell speech of 1961 would offer a stinging critique the cost of war and warmongering on society. But in 1938, Mussolini exhorted their personal sacrifice for the country, shouting to a crowd: "Guns or butter, which do we choose?" and the crowd shouted back, "Guns!"[292]

The United States Congress had similarly chosen guns over butter when it passed The Selective Service Act of 1917, declaring a state of "emergency" and authorizing President Wilson to "draft into the military service....five hundred thousand enlisted men," from American society. Wilson had not mentioned Germany or war once in his December 1916 State of the Union Address, but in December 1917, he insisted that American society must sacrifice at home in order to help dismantle empire in Europe and Asia:

> Let there be no misunderstanding. Our present and immediate task is to win the war, and nothing shall turn us aside from it until it is accomplished. Every power and resource we possess, whether of men, of money, or of materials, is being devoted and will continue to be devoted to that purpose until it is achieved. Those who desire to bring peace about before that purpose is achieved I counsel to carry their advice elsewhere. We will not entertain it. We shall regard the war as won only when the German people say to us, through properly accredited representatives, that they are ready to agree to a settlement based upon justice and the reparation of the wrongs their rulers have done. They have done a wrong to

---

[290] Ibid., Kindle locations 2931-2935.
[291] Farrell, *Mussolini*, Kindle Locations 9027-9030.
[292] "Signor Mussolini's Speeches on the Crisis," *Bulletin of International News* 15, no. 20 (1938), 14-16, http://www.jstor.org/stable/25642338.

Belgium which must be repaired. They have established a power over other lands and peoples than their own--over the great Empire of Austria-Hungary, over hitherto free Balkan states, over Turkey, and within Asia--which must be relinquished.

Society had to sacrifice, according to Wilson, who had campaigned as a peace candidate, for the good of the expanding American Corporate-Fascist empire.

The United States has been expanding since its founding. When Manifest Destiny reached the Pacific Coast, the U.S. sought lands and resources in Mexico, Cuba, the Philippines, and Central America. While U.S. society is mostly isolationist, economics has repeatedly reshaped society to look outward and exert force. During the rise of Nazism, literary and social critic Walter Benjamin observed:

> Imperialistic war is a rebellion of technology which collects, in the form of 'human material,' the claims to which society has denied its natural material. Instead of draining rivers, society directs a human stream into a bed of trenches; instead of dropping seeds from airplanes, it drops incendiary bombs over cities; and through gas warfare the aura is abolished in a new way.[293]

The aura of social responsibility fades away to a subservience to nationalism that creates values and morals from above, but the ruled take "the morality imposed upon them more seriously than" do the rulers themselves,[294] who often violate public morals—typically with impunity. Mussolini, Benjamin, and the arichitects

---

[293] Walter Benjamin, "The Work of Art in the Age of Mechanical Reproduction." In: *Illuminations*, edited by Hannah Arendt, translated by Harry Zohn, from the 1935 essay, (New York: Schocken Books, 1969).
[294] Max Horkhiemer and Theodor W. Adorno, *Dialectic of Enlightenment*, (Palo Alto: Stanford University Press, 2007).

of Manifest Destiny understood Auguste Comte's adage that economic, cultural, and social conditions each affect the others and that social consensus can only change with intellectual progress or concerted efforts of propaganda.[295] Edward Bernays described the process as the "conscious and intelligent manipulation of the organized habits and opinions of the masses," as an "important element in democratic society."[296] Bernays admitted that those who mastered this manipulation of society constituted an invisible ruling power who govern as hegemons; we are governed, our minds molded, our tastes formed by these propagandists, according to Bernays, for our own good and in order to organize the nation's affairs through a logical and smoothly functioning society.

U.S. Department of Justice official James Stewart Martin warned in 1950 of the growing power of economic giants in transnational trade where United States authorities had become directly involved in activities that were formerly considered outside government purview. The activities of the socially irresponsible government resembled a pattern of socially irresponsible corporate conduct that benefited big business at the expense of society as a whole.[297] While President Johnson later attempted to alleviate poverty and improve general well-being with his Great Society project, the war machine sabotaged the liberal plan throughout the Johnson presidency, as he embroiled the country in the tragic Vietnam War.[298] The more Johnson

---

[295] Oscar Haac, *The Correspondence of John Stuart Mill and Auguste Comte*, (London: Routledge, 1994), 22.

[296] Edward Bernays, *Propaganda*, (Ig Publishing. Kindle Edition, 2004), p. 37.

[297] James Stewart Martin, *All Honorable Men: The Story of the Men on Both Sides of the Atlantic Who Successfully Thwarted Plans to Dismantle the Nazi Cartel System*, (New York: Open Road Integrated Media, 2016), Kindle locations 4848-4853.

[298] Walter Mondale, *The Good Fight: A Life in Liberal Politics*, (New York: Simon & Schuster, 2010), 89.

pursued his reformation of American society through legislation such as the 24th Amendment, the Civil Rights Act, the Water Quality Act, the Economic Opportunity Act, the Food Stamp Act, and the Elementary and Secondary Education Act, the more the war and war propaganda encroached on the American consciousness.[299] Daniel Ellsberg eventually revealed the depth and scope of the dishonesty of the Pentagon and government on the American people.[300] As a result, only 20 percent of Americans now rate Johnson as an above-average president, lower than Jimmy Carter or George W. Bush, and few know that the building housing the United States Department of Education bears Johnson's name; the director of the LBJ Library Mark Updegrove recently commented that Johnson "left the presidency under the dark cloud of Vietnam, and it has taken us this long to maybe finally see the forest for the trees," but the "laws he put in place were transformative."[301] Even before he left office, though, Johnson realized that history would define his legacy not by his aggressive social legislative agenda but by his vicious and unwinnable war.[302] Johnson's recklessness reminds us of Eisenhower's admonition that each tax dollar spent on military armaments is not available to spend on social programs. Martin Luther King, Jr. offered the clear-eyed and poetic critique that "If America's soul becomes totally poisoned, part of the autopsy must read 'Vietnam.'"[303]

---

[299] Julian E. Zelizer, *The Fierce Urgency of Now: Lyndon Johnson, Congress, and the Battle for the Great Society*, (New York: Penguin, 2016).

[300] Margaret Susca, "From the Pentagon Papers to Trump: How the Government Gained the Upper Hand Against Leakers," Salon, 17 June 2017.

[301] Albert R. Hunt, "Remembering L.B.J. for More Than Vietnam," *New York Times*, 14 April 2014.

[302] Jeffrey K. Smith, B*ad Blood: Lyndon B. Johnson, Robert F. Kennedy and the Tumultuous 1960s*, (New York: Author House, 2010), 288.

[303] Matt Pearce, "Martin Luther King Jr. Fought for More Than Civil Rights. This Was the Protest Less Remembered, *Los Angeles Times*, 16 January 2017.

Richard Nixon and Henry Kissinger were at work escalating and prolonging the Vietnam War before Nixon even took office,[304] and once in office Nixon immediately undermined the Great Society project with a cynical "law and order" project and a racist war on drugs.[305] 40 years later, the war on drugs has executed 40 million arrests and destroyed lives, families, and entire communities all over the country.[306] But the powers that be continue the debacle, with Attorney General Sessions seeking to expand it in 2017 because it strengthens law enforcement and creates billions in profits for related corporate businesses. In 2010, U. S. drug czar Gil Kerlikowske conceded to the Associated Press that "In the grand scheme," the war on drugs "has not been successful," and over four decades later, "the concern about drugs and drug problems is, if anything, magnified, intensified,"[307] despite the decades-long campaign.

In a campaign to bring back a new Manifest Destiny, the Trump administration seeks to convince Americans that current conditions require a change in society into one that condones barring Muslims from entering the country, slashing regulations on business, outlawing abortion, jailing journalists, deporting millions of workers, and torturing suspects.[308] And, like Mussolini, Trump hopes that Americans either embrace this collective—fascistic—identity or face ridicule, ostracism,

---

[304] Colin Schulz, "Nixon Prolonged Vietnam War for Political Gain—And Johnson Knew About It, Newly Unclassified Tapes Suggest," Smithsonian, 18 March 2013.

[305] Tom LoBiance "Report: Aide Says Nixon's War on Drugs Targeted Blacks, Hippies," CNN, 24 March 2016.

[306] Mike Brickner, "40 Years and Over 40 Million Arrests Later, War on Drugs Still Harming Our Communities," ACLU of Ohio 16 June 2011.

[307] Associated Press, "After 40 years, $1 trillion, US War on Drugs Has Failed to Meet Any of Its Goals," Fox World, 13 May 2010.

[308] Michael Kinsley, "Trump Is Actually a Fascist," Washington Post, 9 December 2016.

prosecution, or even imprisonment in Guantanamo.[309] An early academic critique of the Trump victory found that American society, as frustrated as interwar Italy, had chosen "a president who promised to overturn customs, protocols, and institutions of government," rejecting any continuity of what had previously seemed to be normal.[310] The more lies Trump told during the campaign, the more adolescent, bigoted, defiant, and sexist his behavior, the more he rose in the polls. Fortunately, a few months into the incompetent Trump presidency, more and more Americans are ignoring or rejecting Trump's divisive and alarmist propaganda,[311] so the Gustave Le Bon style Trump-mobocracy project is not progressing as hoped.[312]

There are and always have been alternatives and opposition to Fascism in the United States; San Francisco Supervisor Jeff Sheehy recently called for local legislation prohibiting San Francisco Police from removing passengers from airplanes overbooked by airlines.[313] Sheehy's efforts began two days after United Airlines and Chicago Airport security violently ejected a paying passenger from a plane in route to Kentucky in April of 2017.[314] Dozens of fellow passengers audibly protested as the officers forcibly removed David Dao, a 69-year-old physician returning home to his practice, and dragged him through the aisle. Several passengers recorded the incident with their cellphones

[309] Carol Rosenberg, "What Will President Trump Do with Guantánamo?" *Miami Herald*, 11 November 2016.
[310] Tony Michels, "Donald Trump and the Triumph of Antiliberalism," *Jewish Social Studies* 22, no. 3 (2017): 186. doi:10.2979/jewisocistud.22.3.11.
[311] Tim Marcin, "Donald Trump's Latest Approval Plunges to New Low (Even Before Comey Memo Surfaced)," *Newsweek*, 17 May 2017.
[312] Robert Zaretsky, "Donald Trump and the Myth of Mobocracy," *Atlantic*, 27 July 2016.
[313] "After United Fiasco, SFPD Urged to Stay Out of Airline Overbooking Disputes," *CBS San Francisco*, 12 April 2017.
[314] Corky Siemasko, "David Dao, Doctor Dragged Off Plane, Files Court Papers Demanding United Airlines Preserve Evidence," 13 April 2017.

and posted the videos of the bloodied Dao to social media, where the files went viral. United Airlines CEO Oscar Munoz initially responded by blaming Dao for being "disruptive and belligerent," and in an internal email, Munoz assured United employees that he would "emphatically stand behind all of" them.[315]

Munoz' callousness only incited more public outrage, forcing him to amend his remarks with an evasive apology the next day: "I apologize for having to re-accommodate these customers. Our team is moving with a sense of urgency to work with the authorities and conduct our own detailed review of what happened." This tepid response from United, however, further aggravated the public reaction, causing a second apology from Munoz 24 hours later: "Like you, I continue to be disturbed by what happened on this flight and I deeply apologize to the customer forcibly removed and to all the customers aboard," concluding: "No one should ever be mistreated this way."[316] Four days after the incident, Dao had contracted an attorney, who filed court papers demanding that United preserve and protect all evidence and alleging that the force was excessive, requiring that Dao undergo reconstructive surgery for injuries.[317] The disgust of American society by the abuse of authority and excessive use of force was so prominent as to cause Wall Street to react with United Airlines stock losing more than $1 billion in value.[318] In the end, the same society that allows the Corporate-Fascist capitalism that forcefully asserts property rights over human

---

[315] Matt Rosoff, "United CEO Doubles Down in Email to Employees," CNBC, 10 April 2017.

[316] Sara Gonzales, "United CEO Takes a Second Stab at an Apology, Contradicts Email to Employees." *The Blaze*, 11 April 2017.

[317] Emily Shugerman, "United Airlines: David Dao Will Need Reconstructive Surgery after Suffering Concussion, Broken Nose and Lost Teeth, Says His Lawyer," *The Independent*, 13 April 2017.

[318] Lucinda Shen, "United Airlines Stock Drops $1.4 Billion After Passenger-Removal Controversy," *Fortune*, 11 April 2017.

rights ultimately condemned the authoritarianism as unacceptably excessive.

Some suggest a universal basic income in order to ensure that each and all in society can live with security and dignity, with the financial means to avoid authoritarian business relations and employers. Former Service Employees International Union President Andy Stern argues that the universal basic income would stabilize the economy, protect workers from the disruption of being replaced by technology, reduce income and wealth inequality, and thereby reinvent the American Dream.[319] The proposal is not new, but it is gaining in popularity, even amongst libertarians, who realize that universal basic income would be "less expensive, less bureaucratic, less prone to political opportunism, and less paternalistic and invasive than our present welfare state."[320] Rutger Bregman goes even further by imagining a utopia in which universal basic income eradicates poverty and reduces the work week to 15 hours, thus increasing leisure time and happiness.[321]

---

[319] Andrew Stern with Lee Kravitz, *Raising the Floor: How a Universal Basic Income Can Renew Our Economy and Rebuild the American Dream*, (New York: Public Affairs, 2016).

[320] Matt Zwolinski, "Property Rights, Coercion, and the Welfare State: The Libertarian Case for a Basic Income for All," *The Independent Review* 19, no. 4 (2015): 516, http://www.jstor.org/stable/24563066.

[321] Rutger Bregman, *Utopia for Realists: How We Can Build the Ideal World*, (New York: Little, Brown and Company, 2017).

Privacy

"The right of the people to be secure in their persons...shall not be violated."
  —United States Constitution Fourth Amendment

"Everything within the state, and nothing outside the state."
  —Benito Mussolini

"Life is complicated enough without having a bunch of senators deciding what we should do in the privacy of our own homes.
  —Barbara Boxer

Mussolini worked as a paid British spy in Italy while still a journalist in 1917 before pursuing his political career. He promised to publish pro-war propaganda (Italy and England were allies in the first world war), surveil politics in Milan, and send Italian army veterans to beat anti-war protestors.[322] Once in power, his Black Shirt Legion proved as invasive, unprincipled, and ruthless as the Stasi would be decades later in East Germany.[323] And though Fascism "energetically" respected the fundamental importance of "private property," it afforded no similar respect for individual privacy.[324] The anti-fascist publication *Il Mondo* opined that for "Fascism the possession of power is not enough: it wants possession of the private conscience of all citizens...."[325] So, there is no need to discuss individual privacy in the Fascist State if the Fascist State possesses the very conscience of each

---

[322] Tom Kington, "Recruited by MI5: the name's Mussolini. Benito Mussolini," *The Guardian*, 13 October 2009.
[323] Robert Strayer, "Communism and Fascism," *The Cambridge World History*. (Cambridge: Cambridge University Press, 2015), pp. 420-441.
[324] Farrell, *Mussolini*. Kindle locations 7065-7068.
[325] Ibid., Kindle locations 3169-3172.

and every citizen. Similarly, Mussolini repeatedly explained that everything was to be inside the state with nothing outside the state. Such an openly totalitarian philosophy militates against even the notion of individual privacy, especially the prospect of an individual or an entity keeping any matter private from the Fascist State itself.

At the same time as Mussolini's first run for office, United States Attorney General A. Mitchell Palmer and a very young J. Edgar Hoover launched a series of raids on "suspected radicals," that quickly devolved into what the FBI's own archives now describes as a "nightmare, marked by poor communications, planning, and intelligence about who should be targeted and how many arrest warrants would be needed," and the constitutionality of the entire operation was questioned at the time, so that "Palmer and Hoover were roundly criticized for the plan and for their overzealous domestic security" operations efforts.[326] Some recent scholars trace forward from the Palmer Raids to the current overuse of national security letters by federal agents to demand—without judicial warrant—that businesses, telecommunication providers, and even librarians disclose the private information of customers or patrons while the recipient of the letter cannot tell anyone at all that the government is seeking the information.[327] The 2007 FBI Archives article on the Palmer Raids concludes: "Director Mueller has said, we realize that the FBI will be judged not just on how well it protects the nation, but also on how well it protects our nation's constitutional freedoms along the way."[328] Many civil society organizations have been

---

[326] Archives, "A Byte out of History: The Palmer Raids," Federal Bureau of Investigation, 28 December 2007.

[327] Christopher P. Banks, "National Security Letters and Diminishing Privacy Rights," in *The Day That Changed Everything"*, (New York: Palgrave Macmillan, 2009), 91-102.

[328] Archives, op. cit.

monitoring the national security letter invasions, though, including the conservative Heritage Foundation.[329] The numbers themselves illustrate the abuse; the Office of the Inspector General of the Department of Justice found 84 possible violations out of about 50,000 requests in 2008 alone. While 84 "possible violations" out of 50,000 letters seems a reasonably low percentage, the number is likely understated given that the investigation is essentially self-reporting. What should alarm us all is the fact that the FBI is issuing 50,000 such letters in a year, letters that are supposedly crucial "to protect against international terrorism or clandestine intelligence activities," but which are not to be issued in investigations of U.S. persons "conducted solely upon the basis of activities protected by the first amendment to the Constitution of the United States," as the Foreign Intelligence Surveillance Act codifies, but courts usually interpret these laws in favor of the government, not the citizen as target.[330] Logically, if the FBI issues 50,000 counter-terrorism investigation letters in a year, we should see at least hundreds of arrests, but most alleged plots look more like extreme entrapment of incompetents who would be incapable of execution without inordinate guidance and assistance from the FBI handlers themselves.[331]

As for a commitment to privacy, the Fourth Amendment provides for that "The right of the people to be secure in their persons, houses, papers, and effects, against unreasonable searches and seizures, shall not be violated," and that "no Warrants shall issue, but upon probable cause, supported by Oath or affirmation, and particularly describing the place to be

---

[329] Andrew Grossman and Charles Stimson, "National Security Letters: Three Important Facts," Heritage Foundation, 14 March 2008.

[330] Jodie Liu, "The Latest FISC Opinion: A Summary," *Lawfare*, 29 August 2014.

[331] Trevor Aaronson, *The Terror Factory: Inside the FBI's Manufactures War on Terrorism*, (New Jersey: Ig Publishing, 2013).

searched, and the persons or things to be seized." Currently, 15 U.S.C. § 45 authorizes the Federal Trade Commission to prevent "unfair methods of competition in or affecting commerce and unfair or deceptive acts or practices in or affecting commerce," and with respect to privacy, the FTC enforces privacy promises made by businesses to consumers through the Privacy Act of 1974 (5 U.S.C. § 552a), the Gramm-Leach-Bliley Act (15 U.S.C. §§ 6801-6809), the Fair Credit Reporting Act (15 U.S.C. § 1681 et seq.), and the Children's Online Privacy Protection Act (15 U.S.C. §§ 6501-6506). Remarkably, however, extreme conservative jurists such as Robert Bork continue to argue in writings, and at Bork's unsuccessful Senate confirmation hearing for a seat on the Supreme Court, that the Constitution does not protect privacy because the founders did not mention the term in the document; at his hearing, Bork repeated his criticisms that landmark Supreme Court decisions such as *Griswold v. Connecticut* and *Roe v. Wade* were "unprincipled" and "utterly specious" and "intellectually empty."[332]

The national security and surveillance state agrees with Bork. In the United States of 2017, we have 17 "intelligence" agencies,[333] but this does not include private contractors or other commercial interests that require personal data from consumers in order to complete transactions—especially on the Internet: "Your internet provider can see what websites you visit, when you visit them, and how much time you spend there."[334] During a Spring 2017 town hall meeting in Wisconsin, United States Congressman

---

[332] Anita L. Allen, "Why Does Bork Have Trouble with a Right to Privacy?" *Chicago Tribune*, 29 September 1987.

[333] Nina Agrawal, "There's more than the CIA and FBI: The 17 Agencies That Make up the U.S. Intelligence Community," *Los Angeles Times*, 17 January 2017.

[334] Lint Finley, "The FCC Seems Unlikely to Stop Internet Providers from Selling Your Data," *Wired*, 1 March 2017.

Sensenbrenner defended his recent vote to end the Federal Communication Commission's privacy rule by placing corporate profits and power over consumer rights: "Well," he rationalized, "Nobody's got to use the internet, at all," continuing, "the thing is, if you start regulating the Internet like a utility, if we did that right at the beginning, we would have no internet." Sensenbrenner offered no evidence or even explanation of this odd claim, but he went on to reveal his sympathy not with his real person constituents, but rather with the "internet companies" as constituents, who "have invested an awful lot of money in having almost universal service now." The Congressman concluded with a typical false call to freedom: "My job, I think, is to tell you that you have the opportunity to do it, and then you take it upon yourself to make the choice."[335] But given the level of work, communication, news, entertainment, and commerce that has moved to the Internet, the supposed choice not to use the technology would unfairly limit anyone who opts out, and negotiating individual privacy agreements with a large business is virtually impossible, leaving most Americans at the mercy of the corporate lawyers and in a state of what Ralph Nader refers to as contract peonage.[336]

More disturbing than the vague or one-sided privacy contracts is the reality that in April 2017 President Trump signed Congressman Sensenbrenner's resolution repealing the requirement that Internet service providers obtain informed consent of customers before collecting and selling data about their online activities.[337] The original sponsor of the repeal resolution, Congresswoman Marsha Blackburn of Tennessee,

---

[335] Kate Cox, "Killing Privacy is Fine Because 'Nobody's Got to Use the Internet' House Rep Says." *Consumerist*, 17 April 2017.
[336] Ralph Nader, "Contract Peonage," *The Nader Page*, 31 May 2011.
[337] Steve Lohr, "Trump Completes Repeal of Online Privacy Protections from Obama Era," *New York Times*, 3 April 2017.

reasoned that "Companies have a financial incentive to handle your personal data properly because to do otherwise would significantly impair their financial standing."[338] But "consumers should not have to pay for the right to be left alone," as columnist Hiawatha Bray commented, and the repealed rule "was a reasonable attempt to restore 'none of your business' as the default setting for the Internet."[339] The Electronic Frontier Foundation warns that, based on secret or corporate surveillance, "the next time you try to board a plane, watch out—you might be turned away after being mistakenly placed on a government watch list, or be forced to open your email in the security line."[340]

Perhaps most disturbing of all, and not even imagined by George Orwell, is the collection of personal biometric data into the FBI Next Generation Identification database.[341] In the related Domain Awareness System with its 3,000 surveillance cameras, any "person who lives and works in lower Manhattan would be under constant surveillance," by any law enforcement official or contractor who has access to the system.[342] No court has yet addressed the question of the government collecting facial recognition data in public, and ongoing Carnegie Mellon University research highlights some of the power and dangers. The CMU research team cross-referenced social media profile photographs with photographs on ostensibly anonymous dating

---

[338] Mike Snider, ISPs Can Now Collect and Sell Your data: What to Know about Internet privacy rules, *USA Today*, 4 April 2017.

[339] Hiawatha Bray, "Internet Privacy, Such as It Is, Loses Yet Another Defense. Sad!," *Boston Globe*, 29 March 2017.

[340] Surveillance Self-Defense Project, "Privacy Topics," Electronic Frontier Foundation.

[341] "Comments on FBI's Proposed Exemption from the Privacy Act for Next Generation Identification System." Center for Democracy & Technology, 2017.

[342] "Biometric Security Poses Huge Privacy Risks: Without Explicit Safeguards, Your Personal Biometric Data Are Destined for a Government Database," *Scientific American*, 1 January 2014.

sites in one experiment; in a separate experiment, the researchers identified students on campus based on their online social media photographs; and the team eventually designed a smartphone app that combined online and offline data to overlay private and personal information onto the facial photographs.[343] For those who do not post photos on social media, CMU researchers developed a camera that can collect iris scans of unwitting persons in a crowd: "There's no X-marks-the-spot. There's no place you have to stand. Anywhere between six and 12 meters, it will find you, it will zoom in and capture both irises and full face."[344] The private citizen is an endangered species in the new Corporate-Fascist United States.

Fortunately, there are socially responsible civil society institutions that are technically savvy enough to monitor surveillance technology. The Electronic Frontier Foundation recommends standards for industry and has evaluated AT&T, Verizon, and WhatsApp as behind others in the tech industry in defending customers, while Adobe, Apple, CREDO, Dropbox, Sonic, Wickr, Wikimedia, Wordpress.com, and Yahoo lead the industry in customer loyalty. The EFF evaluation criteria include the following:

1. *Industry-Accepted Best Practices.* This is a combined category that measures companies on three criteria (which were each listed separately in prior years' reports):
Does the company require the government to obtain a warrant from a judge before handing over the content of user communications?

[343] "More Than Facial Recognition," Carnegie Mellon University.
[344] Mike Blake, "Long-Range Iris Scanning Is Here: An Engineering Professor at Carnegie Mellon Says He's Invented Technology That Can Identify Someone from Across the Room with the Precision of a Fingerprint," *The Atlantic*, 13 May 2015.

Does the company publish a transparency report, i.e. regular, useful data about how many times governments sought user data and how often the company provided user data to governments?

Does the company publish law enforcement guides explaining how they respond to data demands from the government?

Companies must fulfill all three criteria in order to receive credit.

2. *Tell users about government data requests.* To earn a star in this category, Internet companies must promise to tell users when the U.S. government seeks their data unless prohibited by law, in very narrow and defined emergency situations, or unless doing so would be futile or ineffective. Notice gives users a chance to defend themselves against overreaching government demands for their data. The best practice is to give users prior notice of such demands, so that they have an opportunity to challenge them in court. We have thus adjusted our criterion from prior years. We now require that the company provide advance notice to users except when prohibited by law or in an emergency and that the company also commit to providing delayed notice after the emergency has ended or when the gag has been lifted.

3. *Publicly disclose the company's data retention policies.* This category awards companies that disclose how long they maintain data about their users that isn't accessible to the user—specifically including logs of users' IP addresses and deleted content—in a form accessible to law enforcement. If the retention period may vary for technical or other reasons, the company must disclose that fact and should publish an approximate average or typical range, along with an upper bound, if any.

4. *Disclose the number of times governments seek* the removal of user content or accounts and how often the

company complies. Transparency reports are now industry standard practices. EFF believes that companies' responsibility to be transparent includes not only disclosing when governments demand user data, but also how often governments seek the removal of user content or the suspension of user accounts and how often the company complies with such demands. EFF awards a star in this category to companies that regularly publish this information, either in their transparency report or in another similarly accessible form. Companies should include formal legal process as well as informal government requests in their reporting, as government censorship takes many forms.

5. *Pro-user public policies*: opposing backdoors. Every year, EFF dedicates one category to a public policy position of a company. For three years, EFF acknowledged companies working publicly to update and reform the Electronic Communications Privacy Act. Last year, EFF noted companies who publicly opposed mass surveillance. This year, given the reinvigorated debate over encryption, EFF is asking companies to take a public position against the compelled inclusion of deliberate security weaknesses or other compelled back doors. This could be in a blog post, in a transparency report, by publicly signing a coalition letter, or through another public, official, written format. EFF expects this category to continue to evolve, so that EFF can track industry players across a range of important privacy issues.[345]

Given the power of private tech companies in the modern society and economy, corporate policies and practice are key to individual freedom and privacy.

---

[345] Electronic Frontier Foundation, "Who Has Your Back? Government Data Requests 2015," Evaluation Criteria, 2015, https://www.eff.org/who-has-your-back-government-data-requests-2015#executive-summary.

Arts

"The art of war is of vital importance to the State."
 —Sun Tzu

"War is beautiful...it enriches a flowering meadow with the fiery orchids of machine guns."
 —Filippo Tomasso Marinetti

"I am happy to be alive, as long as I can paint."
 —Frida Kahlo

To some, the ultimate Fascist act of warfare is itself art, as Mussolini collaborator Marinetti describes in his 1909 futurist manifesto: "We want to glorify war—the only cure for the world—militarism, patriotism, the destructive gesture of the anarchists, the beautiful ideas which kill, and contempt for woman." The ease with which Marinetti includes misogyny is consistent with modern patriarchy. The next sentence adds to the mayhem: "We want to demolish museums and libraries, fight morality, feminism and all opportunist and utilitarian cowardice." Part of the totalitarian Fascist project included an attempt to use art to mobilize the masses into creating a new society through culture, a culture that was modernist, futurist, and orderly.[346] Fascism attracted *avanguardisti* artists such as painter Mario Sironi, much favored by Mussolini himself, who sought to synthesize the classic with the modern, much as Mussolini sought to do in Fascist politics. Sironi and Mussolini's mistress Sarfatti promoted a *Novecento* movement to further Fascist literature and art in order to a create "modern classicity" and "revolutionary

---

[346] Kate Flint, "Art and the Fascist Régime in Italy," *Oxford Art Journal Volume 3* (2), Issue 2, October 1980, 49-54.

restoration" to inspire the masses, but Mussolini ultimately disapproved of Sarfatti's "shameless" promotion efforts: "This attempt to make people think that the artistic position of Fascism is represented by your *Novecento* is both futile and a lie..."[347] Meanwhile, Alberto Moravia's first novel, *Gli Indifferenti*, mocking bourgeois life of some in Italy met with much party approval, and architect Giuseppe Terragni's masterpiece *Casa del Fascio* in Como exemplified the new Fascist modern, futurist version of classic Italian building with its courtyard borrowed from ancient villas of the Roman Empire.

Art can protest society, reflect it, or parody it. In Puritan New England, piety demanded humility, chastity, and respect for hierarchy, which included respect for patriarchy, as Anne Bradstreet demonstrates in her poem "To my Dear and Loving Husband,"

> If ever two were one, then surely we.
> If ever man were lov'd by wife, then thee;
> If ever wife was happy in a man,
> Compare with me ye women if you can.
>
> I prize thy love more than whole Mines of Gold,
> Or all the riches that the East doth hold.
> My love is such that Rivers cannot quench,
> Nor ought but love from thee, give recompence.
>
> Thy love is such I can no way repay,
> The heavens reward thee manifold I pray.
> Then while we live, in love lets so persevere,
> That when we live no more, we may live ever.

Bradstreet seems entirely repressed by 21st century standards, but the fact that she, a woman, would write creatively at all was

---

[347] Nicholas Farrell, *Mussolini*, Kindle locations 6349-6385.

considered daring in her day. "The Puritans believed that God should be observed in everything and everything should lead the believer back to him, but Bradstreet tended to stop in the middle of the process."[348] Still, Bradstreet's poem celebrates "the process of finding one's place, of confirming one's properly grateful and lovingly dependent relationship to God's supremacy," here on earth.[349]

Calvin Coolidge shares a similar Christian vision of life, divinity, and art in his autobiography:

Every reaction in the universe is a manifestation of His presence. Man was revealed as His son, and nature as the hem of His garment, while through a common Fatherhood we are all embraced in a common brotherhood. The spiritual appeal of music, sculpture, painting and all other art lies in the revelation it affords of the Divine beauty.[350]

His first address to Congress, in 1923, concluded with his own artistic flourish, invoking faith, rejecting war, and calling instead for a better use of moral power:

The world has had enough of the curse of hatred and selfishness, of destruction and war. It has had enough of the wrongful use of material power. For the healing of the nations there must be good will and charity, confidence and peace. The time has come for a more practical use of moral power, and more reliance upon the principle that right makes its own might. Our authority among the nations must be represented by justice and mercy. It is necessary not only to have faith,

[348] Ileana Vesa, "The Complementary Poetic Vision of Anne Bradstreet," *Scientific Journal of Humanistic Studies* 6, no. 10 (2014), 85.
[349] Anne G. Myles, "Queerly Lamenting Anne Bradstreet," *Women's Studies* 43, no. 3 (2014), 353.
[350] Calvin Coolidge, *Autobiography of Calvin Coolidge*, (New York: Walking Through the Word), Kindle locations 575-577.

but to make sacrifices for our faith. The spiritual forces of the world make all its final determinations. It is with these voices that America should speak. Whenever they declare a righteous purpose there need be no doubt that they will be heard. America has taken her place in the world as a Republic--free, independent, powerful.[351]

The next year Coolidge would become the first president to perform in talking newsreels played before feature films in theaters across the nation.[352]

Charlie Chaplin's first talkie performance, *The Great Dictator* of 1940, Chaplin artfully mocks the rise of Hitler to earthly supremacy in a way that most journalists would not dare do at the time. Like a skilled performing artist, Chaplin juggles "countless balls of his pure possibility," while he "fixes its restless circling into a fabric that has little more in common with the causal world than Cloudcuckooland has with the gravitation of Newtonian physics," instead creating a "utopia of an existence…free of the burden of being-one's-self."[353] Similarly, Walter Lipmann argued for promoting art as a way of "admitting us to the inner life of others," and as "a medium by which barbarous lusts find civilized expression" because only "art can open up the springs from which conduct flows" and then "penetrate where most of us can only observe."[354] He continued to argue that "the life and so the politics of a nation sink into a

---

[351] Calvin Coolidge, "First Annual Message," December 6, 1923, Online by Gerhard Peters and John T. Woolley, *The American Presidency Project*. http://www.presidency.ucsb.edu/ws/?pid=29564.

[352] Jerry L. Wallace, "A Biographical Sketch of Calvin Coolidge," Coolidge Foundation, 2017, https://coolidgefoundation.org/presidency/a-biographical-sketch-of-calvin-coolidge/.

[353] Theodor W. Adorno, "Chaplin Times Two," trans John MacKay, *The Yale Journal of Criticism* 9.1 (1996), 60.

[354] Walter Lipmann, *A Preface to Politics*, (New York Firework Press. Kindle Edition, 2016), 57-58.

barren routine," without art, and he theorized that any "country populated by pure logicians and mathematical scientists would…produce few inventions." Lipmann concluded that America would do well to "remember the close alliance of art, science and politics in Athens, in Florence and Venice at their zenith."[355]

Franklin Delano Roosevelt included art in his New Deal. The Public Works of Art Project hired 3,749 artists (including Jackson Pollock and Mark Rothko) and created 15,663 sculptures, murals, paintings, prints, and crafts for display in government buildings around the country beginning in 1934, paying an average of $75.59 per artwork.[356] Roosevelt endured much criticism for all of the New Deal projects and worried that he could not defend "a lot of young enthusiasts painting Lenin's head on the Justice Building."[357] The PWAP instructed artists to portray the "American scene," so the "art they produced was rather conservative," but some conservatives scoured the public art for signs of hidden socialist messages: "They'd look at two blades of grass and see a hammer and sickle."[358] When an early mural project on San Francisco Coit Tower included Bernard Zakein's depiction of Marx's *Das Kapital* on the shelf of the San Francisco Public Library, the authorities locked up the work to protect the good people of California from the "communist propaganda."[359] The First American Artists' Congress responded by calling for both continued government funding for art and freedom from "censorship of the artist's concept or suppression

[355] Ibid., 59.
[356] Jerry Adler, "1934: Art of the New Deal," *Smithsonian Magazine*, June 2009.
[357] Kevin Starr, *The Dream Endures: California Enters the 1940s*, (Oxford: Oxford University Press, 2002).
[358] Adler, op. cit.
[359] Lloyd Bradley and Thomas Eaton, *Book of Secrets*, (Riverside, New Jersey: Andrews McMeel Publishing, 2005), p. 58.

of the finished work."[360] Art critic David D'Arcy argued that the German, Italian, Soviet, and American governments all "mandated and funded art when image-building served nation-building at its most extreme.... The four countries rallied their citizens with images of rebirth and regeneration."[361] Looking back on the arts and other public projects decades later, Ronald Reagan oddly commented that "Fascism was really the basis for the New Deal."[362]

The American Empire adopted a formal arts policy as part of the Cold War battle for cultural hegemony around the globe.[363] President Eisenhower was an amateur artist, creating over 250 paintings, most landscapes of his family farm in Gettysburg, Pennsylvania. He also painted portraits of his granddaughter, himself, and Presidents Lincoln and Washington. Eisenhower joked that his paintings "would have burned...a long time ago if [he] weren't the president of the United States."[364] Nevertheless, Eisenhower proposed a federal commission to promote the arts in 1955.[365] Staunch anti-communist John F. Kennedy began a speech on the arts by invoking "national strength," and quickly moved to a discussion of American poet Robert Frost, whom Kennedy lauded because Frost "knew the midnight as well as

---

[360] Matthew Baigell, Julia Williams, *Artists Against War and Fascism: Papers of the First American Artists' Congress, Volume 1936*, (New Brunswick, New Jersey: Rutgers University Press, 1986), p. 34.

[361] David Boaz, "Hitler, Mussolini, Roosevelt," Cato Institute, 2007.

[362] Lee Lescaze, "Reagan Still Sure Some in New Deal Espoused Fascism," *Washington Post*, 24 December 1981.

[363] Donna M. Binkiewicz, *Federalizing the Muse: United States Arts Policy and the National Endowment for the Arts*, 1965-1980, (Chapel Hill: University of North Carolina Press, 2005).

[364] Raleigh DeGeer Amyx, "Dwight D. Eisenhower: Presidential Painter," American Heritage Blog, 16 May 2016, http://blog.americanheritage1.com/blog/dwight-d-eisenhower-presidential-painter.

[365] Charles S. Clark, "Is Boosting the Status of the Arts a Wise Investment?," *Arts Funding* 4, Issue 39 (1994).

high noon, because he understood the ordeal as well as the triumph of the human spirit, he gave his age strength with which to overcome despair."[366] Kennedy went on to "look forward to a great future for America, a future in which our country will match its military strength with our moral restraint, its wealth with…wisdom, its power with…purpose…an America which commands respect throughout the world not only for its strength but for its civilization as well."[367] JFK thus weaponized arts to fight the Soviets. Two years later, Johnson signed the National Foundation for the Arts and the Humanities, stating that "where there is no vision, the people perish."[368] During Nixon's tenure, funding rose from $8 million to $60 million a year,[369] though he ordered Modern paintings and sculptures removed from American embassies and assessed that "those who are on the Modern art and music kick are 95 percent against us anyway."[370] Reagan sought to defund the NEA and move arts funding away from government and into the private sector.[371] In 2017, the Heritage Foundation and the Republican Study Committee in the House of Representatives urged President Trump and the Congress to eliminate both the National Endowment for the Arts and the National Endowment for the Humanities, largely in order to "deliver a symbolic victory against leftist urban constituencies," in the ongoing culture wars.[372]

---

[366] John F. Kennedy, "Remarks at Amherst College," National Endowment for the Arts, 26 October 1963.
[367] Ibid.
[368] Lyndon B. Johnson: "Remarks at the Signing of the Arts and Humanities Bill.," *The American Presidency Project*, 29 September 1965.
[369] Micah Mattix, "The Myth of JFK and the Arts," *American Conservative*, 26 November 2013.
[370] Christopher Knight, "The NEA works. Why does Trump want to destroy it?" *New York Times*, 16 March 2017.
[371] Irvin Molotsky, "Reagan Expected to Cut Spending for the Arts," *New York Times*, 3 February 1982.
[372] Dana Gioia, "For the Umpteenth Time, the National Endowment for the

The painting hobby of the now retired President George W. Bush is interesting. His most recent works focus on U.S. combat veterans featured in his 2017 book, *Portraits of Courage*. The 192 pages reproduce Bush's oil paintings of those wounded while serving under Bush as Commander in Chief. Bush provides narratives from the veterans describing their injuries and recoveries. In a March 2017 interview with *Time* magazine, Bush explained his artistic goals for the collection:

> I hope civilians realize there's not an ounce of self-pity in these veterans, and I hope that inspires our citizens to overcome their own struggles, whatever they may be. I hope veterans realize that it's courageous to talk about their injuries, including invisible wounds of war like posttraumatic stress.[373]

Unfortunately, Bush was not as thoughtful about starting the wars that displaced, injured, and killed millions.[374]

As for the supposed art or beauty of warfare itself, MSNBC news anchor Brian Williams echoes Marinetti's admiration of militarism over 100 years later when describing the nighttime videos of Raytheon Tomahawk missiles launched at Syria: "We see these beautiful pictures at night from the decks of these two U. S. Navy vessels in the Eastern Mediterranean." Williams then shares that he himself is "tempted to quote the great Leonard Cohen: 'I am guided by the beauty of our weapons.'" Williams adds his own awe of the spectacle, "And they are beautiful pictures of fearsome armaments making for them what is a brief

---

Arts Deserves Its Funding," *New York Times*, 17 February 2017.

[373] Michel Duffy, "George W. Bush Discusses His New Book of Oil Paintings," *Time*, 1 March 2017.

[374] John Tirman, "Bush's War Totals: Bush's War Totals: The Human Cost of Bush's War: 1 Million dead. 4.5 Million displaced. 1 Million to 2 Million Widows. 5 million Orphans," *The Nation*, 29 January 2009.

flight over to this airfield," before Williams finally turns to his guest to ask, "What did they hit?"[375] Williams, here, serves as a parrot of the exact response Raytheon and the military industrial complex had created in its careful public relations campaign to sanitize and beautify warfare, thus elevating American Corporate-Fascism abroad to a deadly art.

Art will be part of the solution too, as it has been. Soon after the 100th day of the Trump administration, author John Altman reminded us of the 1935 cautionary tale *It Can't Happen Here*, in which a fascist candidate comes to power As Altman saw it, "Now it has happened here. And it continues to happen, week after week," so writers, "along with countless others, scramble to find their footing amid the chaos—and hope that sanity eventually prevails, and rules once again apply."[376] Three days before Trump's inauguration, the *New York Times* published a current review of the classic. The reviewer compares the fictitious Berzelius Windrip, "a blustery populist candidate rising, against all odds," to the 21st century Twitter artist in chief.[377] The art of satire in political dissent in the United States traces back at least to the antiwar movement of 1812, nicknaming army commander Henry Dearborn as "General Quixote," and deriding President Madison as a "foolish elf," an "infatuated Alchymist," a "timorous little monkey," and a "political pimp."[378] *Saturday Night Live* writers should take note. And the recently re-published anti-Fascist art of Si Lewen in "Parade" displays the

---

[375] Brian Williams, "The 11th Hour with Brian Williams," *MSNBC*, 6 April 2017.

[376] John Altman, "Trump Is Stranger Than Fiction: John Altman on Writing Thrillers Today," *Los Angeles Times*, 12 May 2017.

[377] Beverly Gage, "Reading the Classic Novel that Predicted Trump," *New York Times*, 17 January 2017.

[378] Aaron McLean Winter, "The Laughing Doves of 1812 and the Satiric Endowment of Antiwar Rhetoric in the United States," *PMLA* 124, no. 5 (2009): 1564, http://www.jstor.org/stable/25614385.

destruction and inhumanity of war, based on Lewen's experiences landing at Normandy and later liberating the captives and the Buchenwald concentration and death camp. Albert Einstein remarked on the humanity in Lewen's work: "I find it a real merit to counteract the tendencies towards war through the medium of art. Nothing can equal the psychological effect of real art. … Our time needs you and your work!"[379] Once again, Einstein was prescient and wise.

---

[379] Michael Cavna, "'Maus' Creator Art Spiegelman Sheds Light on a Lesser-known Graphic Novel Visionary," *New York Times*, 26 July 2017.

Media

"We need a method if we are to investigate the truth of things."
—René Descartes

"I have abolished the subversive press."
—Benito Mussolini

"Information is a public good, not a commodity."
—Janine Jackson

Mussolini bragged in his autobiography that he had "abolished the subversive press," because he believed that "their only function was to inflame men's minds," so he "sent to confinement" all of the "professional subversives."[380] He went on to claim that not "a day goes by that we do not feel in Italian life how much good has been wrought by these measures against the forces of disintegration, disorder and disloyalty." In its place, Mussolini built pro-Fascist media, which he described in military terms, he "could not use with efficient strength" his strongest convictions without that "modern weapon, capable of all possibilities, ready to arm and to help, good for offense and defense—the newspaper," he needed a daily newspaper, he "hungered for one," and early on he "wanted a newspaper that would hold the city of Milan like a fortress, with editorial articles of such value that they would be reprinted or quoted by every Italian newspaper."[381] Mussolini even garnered a favorable front page headline on Hollywood's *Variety* magazine in September 1927: "Mussolini's Hope in Screen."[382] Mussolini thereby

---

[380] Mussolini, *My Autobiography*, Kindle locations 2211-2217.
[381] Ibid., Kindle locations 426-433.

anticipated media manipulation later used by Nixon, Bush, Trump and advisors such as Roger Ailes, who sensationalized promises and exploited salacious rumors to titillate audiences and draw their attention to a circus of politics that would draw attention to politicians in order to increase their celebrity, which celebrity they used to increase coverage and thereby amplify their message across more and more media outlets in wider and wider coverage of their campaign or agenda, while vilifying opponents with hyperbolic criticisms or fabricated allegations.[383]

American Corporate-Fascism also depends on lack of coverage. Oil magnate and banker David Rockefeller thanked corporate media management for their "discretion," at a 1991 meeting of the Council on Foreign Relations:

> We are grateful to the *Washington Post*, the *NY Times*, *Time Magazine*, and other great publications whose directors have attended our meetings and respected their promises of discretion for almost 40 years.
>
> It would have been impossible for us to develop our plan for the world if we had been subjected to the lights of publicity during those years.
>
> But now the world is more sophisticated and prepared to march towards a world government. The super national sovereignty of an intellectual elite and world bankers is surely preferable to the national auto-determination practiced in past centuries.[384]

---

[382] Janet Bergstrom, "Murnau, Movietone and Mussolini," *Film History* 17, no. 2/3 (2005): 188, http://www.jstor.org/stable/3815590.

[383] Adam Haslett, "Donald Trump, Shamer in Chief, *The Nation*, 24 October 2016.

[384] David Rockefeller, "Quotes," Goodreads, https://www.goodreads.com/author/quotes/9951.David_Rockefeller.

Distraction, too, is key to media manipulation. Mainstream corporate media unwittingly colluded in Trump's Syria distraction away from the debate over the extremely authoritarian Supreme Court nominee Neil Gorsuch, who wrote the *Hobby Lobby* decision that created religious freedom rights for corporations and placed them above privacy and personal rights of employees pursuing access birth control through health insurance policies that employers, such as the fundamentalist Christian Hobby Lobby, happen to fund under the Affordable Care Act. Gorsuch explained his fetish for hierarchy and authority in the corporate retail workplace in stark biblical terms: "All of us face the problem of complicity. All of us must answer for ourselves whether and to what degree we are willing to be involved in the wrongdoing of the other," but religion itself "provides an essential source of guidance both about what constitutes wrongful conduct and the degree to which those who assist others in committing wrongful conduct themselves bear moral culpability.[385] For Gorsuch, then, contraception is "wrongdoing" and the for-profit corporation management that choses to do so can refuse to fund otherwise legally mandated health care. The media under-reported the Hobby Lobby case and Gorsuch's even more troubling lone dissent in the so called "Frozen Trucker" case, in which Gorsuch notoriously ruled that Occupational Safety and Health Administration whistleblower protections did not prevent TransAm Trucking from dismissing a trucker who refused to continue to pull a trailer with malfunctioning brakes in sub-zero temperatures, instead disconnecting the trailer after waiting in vain for hours for the road service that his employer promised was on the way.[386] At

---

[385] Steve Vladeck, 'Hobby Lobby and Executive Power: Gorsuch's Key Rulings," CNN, 1 February 2017.
[386] Jed Shugerman, "Neil Gorsuch and the "Frozen Trucker," *Slate*, 21 March 2017.

the Senate confirmation hearings, Senator Al Franken challenged Gorsuch on the "absurd" inhumanity of the dissent.[387] Unfortunately, however, few American media outlets concentrated on the Gorsuch hearings while Trump first threatened and then launched unilateral military strikes against Syria the very night before the Senate voted to confirm Gorsuch.[388] The strike itself was blatant Fascism and roundly condemned by Russia, Syria, China, *Al Jazeera* and criticized as illegal by Democrats and Republicans in both houses of Congress. Libertarian-leaning United States Senator from Kentucky and 2016 presidential candidate Rand Paul called Trump's attacks unconstitutional: "No matter your view of the merits of engaging in Syria, every member of Congress should stand up today and reclaim our Constitutional authority over war."[389] Most outrageous of all, however, is the fact that Raytheon stock, which Trump owned at the time, jumped 3% after Trump ordered 59 of Raytheon's Tomahawk missiles to attack the Syrian airfield that was the alleged staging ground for chemical attacks, though Assad denied such. Following dangerous advice from the same intelligence establishment that lied the United States into the second Iraq War based on demonstrably false allegations of Weapons of Mass Destruction repeated shamelessly by corporate media, Trump ignored his own wise Twitter advice to President Obama: "The President must get Congressional approval before attacking Syria-big mistake if he does not!" Once in power, Trump could not resist the temptation to abuse the power to create the media distraction that Republican Leader Mitch

---

[387] Evan Halper, "Sen. Al Franken brands Gorsuch as partisan and 'absurd,' " *Los Angeles Times*, 21 March 2017.

[388] Annieli, "More Trump distraction: 60 cruise missiles on Syria ... about which regime change are you concerned?" *DailyKos*, 6 April 2017.

[389] "Rand Paul: 'Illegal' Syrian Strikes Could Have Extreme Ramifications." *Fox News Insider*, 7 April 2017.

McConnell needed to force a change in senate rules in order to drive through the controversial Gorsuch nomination.[390]

Concurrently, perhaps some of the most threatening developments to the abuse of authority of Washington and Wall Street were the unprecedented February 2017 document dumps by Wikileaks revealing CIA cybercrimes. Trump, for various personal reasons, declared the press "the enemy of the people"[391] on several occasions the same month. But CIA Director Pompeo's April 13 (Thomas Jefferson's birthday) bombastic remarks before the Center for Strategic and International Studies expressed the fear the establishment felt about the likelihood of being exposed the way Assange and crew had exposed John Podesta and Wasserman Schulz[392] in 2016: "WikiLeaks walks like a hostile intelligence service and talks like a hostile intelligence service," continuing with ad hominem attacks: "Assange is a narcissist who has created nothing of value [and who] relies on the dirty work of others to make himself famous. He is a fraud—a coward hiding behind a screen."[393] Pompeo's threats, of course, were both dishonest and misdirected in that Assange is clearly too brave and principled to abandon his mission of transparency, but then Assange was not the actual target of Pompeo's craven posturing; the mainstream press was. And, the mainstream press cowered on cue, as veteran independent journalist Glenn Greenwald noted: "Trump's CIA Director stood up in public and explicitly threatened to target free speech rights and press freedoms," in such a menacing and

---

[390] Seung Min Kim, "McConnell tees up nuclear showdown over Gorsuch," *Politico*, 4 April 2017.

[391] David Jackson, "Trump again calls media 'enemy of the people,' " *USA Today*, 24 February 2017.

[392] "18 revelations from Wikileaks' hacked Clinton emails." *BBC News*, 27 October 2016.

[393] Richard Gonzales, "CIA Director Pompeo Denounces WikiLeaks As 'Hostile Intelligence Service,'" *NPR The Two-Way*, 13 April 2017.

effective manner that "it was almost impossible to find even a single U.S. mainstream journalist expressing objections or alarm, because the targets Pompeo chose in this instance are ones they dislike...."[394] Greenwald further pointed to the hypocrisy of Pompeo traveling to Riyadh to award a medal to the Saudi Crown Prince Mohammed bin Nayef bin Abdulaziz al-Saud, Deputy Prime Minister and Minister of Interior[395] shortly before Pompeo accused Assange of "making common cause with dictators."[396] Most disturbing of all, though, is that in answering a question at the CIIS event, Pompeo claimed—contrary to all evidence—that Assange and Wikileaks are "not reporters doing good work trying to keep the American government honest" but instead "are people who are actively recruiting agents to steal American secrets with the sole intention of destroying the American way of life."[397] Pompeo's naked betrayal of the American values of freedom of the press, limited government, and the Ninth Amendment guarantee that the "enumeration in the Constitution, of certain rights, shall not be construed to deny or disparage others retained by the people" could hardly be more stunning in his assumption that he, as director of the same Central Intelligence Agency that experimented with LSD on American citizens without their

---

[394] Glenn Greenwald, "Trump's CIA Director Pompeo, Targeting WikiLeaks, Explicitly Threatens Speech and Press Freedoms," *The Intercept*, 14 April 2017.

[395] "Bin Nayef receives CIA award for 'counter-terrorism,' " *AlJazeera*, 12 February 2017.

[396] Robert Windrem, "CIA Director Pompeo Calls WikiLeaks A 'Hostile Intelligence Service.'" NBC News, 13 April 2017. See also: "Director Pompeo Delivers Remarks at CSIS Remarks as Prepared for Delivery by Central Intelligence Agency Director Mike Pompeo at the Center for Strategic and International Studies," *Central Intelligence Agency News & Information*, 13 April 2017.

[397] "CIA Chief Knocks Assange, But Deems Wikileaks 'Intelligence Agency,'" *YouTube*, 13 April 2017.

consent or even knowledge,[398] should hold the authority to decide what constitutes good reporting or the American way of life.

When mainstream media does not go far enough, more extreme reactionaries employ direct mail or direct email and social media campaigns to tailor their messages aimed at distracting disaffected voters from issues such as unemployment, rising health care costs, and college debt—problems with difficult solutions or solutions that are anathema to the interests of big business. Some of the more common diversionary topics include what Nixon strategist Howard Phillips referred to as "hot button issues" that allow the naming of villains. As mass-mail mogul Richard Viguerie explains, it is difficult to raise money "unless you conjure up an enemy."[399]

Gore Vidal's novel *Empire* narrates a dramatized account of William Randolph Hearst conjuring up the Spanish enemy:

Either the ship had exploded from a spontaneous combustion in the coal-bins, or a floating mine had accidentally hit a bulkhead, or—and this was currently being whispered up and down Printing House Square—Hearst himself had caused the Maine to be blown up so that he could increase the Journal's circulation with his exciting, on-the-spot, coverage of the war. Although Blaise rather doubted that the Chief would go so far as to blow up an American warship, he did think him perfectly capable of creating the sort of emotional climate in which an accident could trigger a war.[400]

Hearst actually did send Frederic Remington to Cuba in 1897, but when Remington informed Hearst that "there will be no war,"

---

[398] Kat Eschner, "What We Know About the CIA's Midcentury Mind-Control Project," *Smithsonian SmartNews*, 13 April 2017.

[399] Krueckl, *Understanding the Roots of Fascism: A Study of the Sources of Fascism Both Within Ourselves and Society*, 167.

[400] Gore Vidal, *Empire*, (New York: Vintage, Kindle Edition, 2011) p. 49.

Hearst responded: "You furnish the pictures and I'll furnish the war."[401] The Congress and the people accepted Hearst's media-conjured enemy, which created the cause for war against Spain, leading to the United States expanding its empire through the Caribbean and all the way across the Pacific to the Philippine Islands.[402] The war would likely have been impossible without the manipulation of public opinion through a jingoistic media.

Organizations such as Media Matters and Fairness and Accuracy in Reporting help to hold irresponsible media outlets accountable to audiences. FAIR's weekly podcast CounterSpin is particularly thorough and analytical.[403] At a media reform conference, Counterspin host Janine Jackson presented a list of important reasons to pursue media reform:

> Media reform is not an academic exercise. Bad media hurts real people. Better media would help real people….
>
> I want truly democratic media because: 45 million Americans don't have health insurance, and many of them believe it's their fault;
>
> I want better media because: black and brown kids go to jail because of what someone read in the paper about 'superpredators';
>
> I want democratic media because: public TV just said that a family with lesbian mothers is unfit to be acknowledged on the network you and I pay for;

---

[401] "The Press: I'll Furnish the War," *Time*, 27 October 1947.
[402] "The Spanish American War: Yellow Journalism," *The Crucible of Empire*, PBS, 1999.
[403] *CounterSpin*, Fairness and Accuracy in Reporting, accessed 18 July 2017, http://fair.org/counterspin-radio/.

I want truly democratic media because: if we had it, tens of thousands of people who have died in Iraq might be alive today.[404]

And the web site of the International Federation of Library Associations and Institutions offers for download a chart with guidelines for "How to Spot Fake News":

CONSIDER THE SOURCE
Click away from the story to investigate the site, its mission and its contact info.

CHECK THE AUTHOR
Do a quick search on the authors. Are they credible? Are they real?

CHECK THE DATE
Reposting old news stories doesn't mean they're relevant to current events.

CHECK YOUR BIASES
Consider if your own beliefs could affect your judgement.

READ BEYOND
Headlines can be outrageous in an effort to get clicks. What's the whole story?

SUPPORTING SOURCES?
Click on those links. Determine if the info given actually supports the story.

IS IT A JOKE?
If it is too outlandish, it might be satire. Research the site and author to be sure.

---

[404] Janine Jackson, "Media Reform," National Conference on Media Reform, 13 May 2005.

ASK THE EXPERTS
Ask a librarian, or consult a fact-checking site.[405]

In critiquing sources, it is important to realize the we are more likely to be manipulated by sources that we typically trust or sources that publish stories that appeal to our own ideology, so we must apply more, not less scrutiny.

---

[405] "How to Spot Fake News," International Federation of Library Associations and Institutions, last updated 20 July 2017, https://www.ifla.org/files/assets/hq/topics/info-society/images/how_to_spot_fake_news.pdf.

Religion

Ἀπόδοτε οὖν τὰ Καίσαρος Καίσαρι καὶ τὰ τοῦ Θεοῦ τῷ Θεῷ

"...seems to me an equal of the gods..."
—Sappho

"My own mind is my church."
—Thomas Paine

"In America, we don't worship government, we worship God."
—Donald J. Trump

Sappho saw the divine in the earthly, while Machiavelli saw the utility of religion in politics,[406] and Mussolini "realized the power of faith to move men,"[407] seeing clearly the advantage of allying himself with official religion, in his case the Roman Catholic church, in order to add a veil of morality to his reign: "Faith in Italy has been strengthened. Fascism gives impulse and vigor to the religion of the country," but he warned that the Fascist government "will never be able for any reason to renounce the sovereign rights of the state and of the functions of the state."[408] And while he offered "general measures to better" the living conditions of the many impoverished clergy who showed "the people the great humane and divine truths," he warned that the "intriguing priest, of course, has to fought."[409] Mussolini boasted regularly of Fascism's alliance with the Vatican: "What is the

---

[406] Nathan Tarcov, "Machiavelli's Critique of Religion," *Social Research: An International Quarterly* 81, number 1, (Spring 2014), 193-216.
[407] Nicholas Farrell, *Mussolini.* (Endeavour Press, Kindle Edition, 2015), locations 3161-3164
[408] Mussolini. *My Autobiography*, Kindle locations 2793-2795).
[409] Ibid., Kindle locations 2669-2671.

truth? It is that a faith openly professed is a sign of strength. I have seen the religious spirit bloom again; churches once more are crowded, the ministers of God are themselves invested with new respect"; he made clear, though, that the Fascist party must come first: "the so-called Catholic party wanted to collaborate by having some members in the government, in the new regime. This collaboration, however, began to lead us through a series of unfortunate misunderstandings," so he "was forced to show the door to the ministers belonging to that party," to protect the hegemony of the Fascist Party.[410] Mussolini continued to negotiate the Lateran Pacts with the Holy See as to the relationship of one to the other, though he remained steadfast to the doctrine of everything with the state and nothing outside the state.[411] By 1931, the parties finally agreed to a compromise on the sensitive subject of the Catholic youth groups, Azione Cattolica, which the Fascist State tolerated so long as they remained locally controlled at the dioceses level and refrained from political, labor, or even athletic activities. The State had already required schoolteachers in 1929 and later university professors to sign oaths of loyalty to Fascism, not Catholicism.[412]

Thomas Hobbes observed that the seed of religion exists in no other living creatures than humans, who seek the true but invisible causes of events by trusting in the authority of others who seem wiser. Living in perpetual anxiety and fear, humans find solace in the existence of gods, or more satisfying a single god. Christians, such as most Americans, especially Republicans, "arrive to the acknowledgment of one infinite, omnipotent, and eternal God...incomprehensible, and above their understanding," and "then confess their definition to be

---

[410] Ibid., Kindle locations 2780-2785.
[411] Albert C. O'Brien, "Benito Mussolini, Catholic Youth, and the Origins of the Lateran Treaties," *Journal of Church and State* 23, no. 1 (1981): 117-29.
[412] Farrell, *Mussolini*, Kindle locations 6148-6165.

unintelligible" in order to honor God "with attributes, of significations, as remote as they can from the grossness of bodies visible."[413] By placing such faith in a deity who, works in mysterious ways, modern Christian Americans submit themselves to a superstitious existence at the whim of a so-called higher power in a mentality that leaves them susceptible to exploitation by charismatic charlatans and demagogues who encourage followers to be "more apt to obedience," of their own authority.[414] Ronald Reagan was not the first American president to associate himself with Christianity, but he may have been the most effective, until George W. Bush. Reagan did, however, begin the regular practice of ending every major speech with the phrase that Richard Nixon first used in April 1973 when apologizing to the American people for his role in the Watergate scandal: "Tonight, I ask for your prayers to help me," he beseeched, "in everything I do throughout the days of my presidency," closing with the prayer, "God bless America and God bless each and every one of you."[415]

President Nixon had formed a pact with Jerry Falwell and Paul Weyrich as part of a Southern Strategy in which the Republicans would deliver Christian-friendly legislation and the evangelicals would deliver votes.[416] The alliance was a natural for the law and order GOP in that evangelicals daily follow dogma and doctrine:

---

[413] Thomas Hobbes, *The Works of Thomas Hobbes*, (Kindle Edition), location 17789.

[414] Thomas Hobbes, *The Complete Works of Thomas Hobbes: Leviathan, Behemoth, The Art of Rhetoric and The Art of Sophistry, A Dialogue Between a Philosopher and a Student, and More*, (Kindle Edition), Kindle locations 17725-17836.

[415] "'God Bless America' in Presidential Speeches Has a Little-Known, Uncomfortable Beginning," *Huffington Post*, 28 January 2014.

[416] Darren Dochuk, "Tea Party American and the Born-Again Politics of the Populist Right," *New Labor Forum* 21, no. 1 (2012): 16.

> The church teaches you to conform. It does not teach you to think for yourself. In fact, quite the contrary, it teaches you to distrust your own thinking processes, submitting yourself instead to the authorities that God put over you (unless they are Democrats of course). They teach you from birth that you are fundamentally wicked, that 'the heart is deceitful above all things,' and that you cannot trust your own judgment. God put your pastor or whoever over you in order to make sure you know what God wants you to do.[417]

The alliance carries through Tea Party politics, and even reluctantly supports the demonstrably un-Christian Donald Trump, months into his failing presidency.[418] "Donald Trump is precisely the type of candidate that would have drawn evangelical Christian voters," explained pollster Steve Mitchell, and though Trump is "certainly not Christ-like, Trump is perceived to be strong and bold; a leader that will help evangelicals navigate a world they believe is too often adrift and too different from what they" should want.[419]

This appeal to hierarchy dates back to the Puritans in the Massachusetts Bay Colony. While in passage in 1630 on the *Arbella*, future Governor John Winthrop delivered what later came to be known as the "City on the Hill" sermon, which Ronald Reagan would quote much later in his own farewell address.[420] Winthrop titled his sermon "A Model of Christian Charity" and explained that "God Almightie in his most holy and

---

[417] Neil Carter, "Without Evangelicals, the Republican Party Would Be History," Patheos, 1 August 2016.

[418] Alexander Nazary, "Evangelicals Stand by Trump, Catholic Journal Attacks Him," *Newsweek*, 17 July 2017.

[419] Steve Mitchell, "Why Evangelicals Support Trump," Real Clear Politics, 6 March 2016.

[420] Peter Bergen, "How Americans learn and don't learn from history," CNN, 3 July 2017.

wise providence," has deigned that "some must be rich" while others be poor; "some high and eminent in power and dignitie;" while others low "and in subjection."[421] Even more important than the Christian charity of the rich in refraining from eating up the poor, the poor and despised must not "rise up against their superiours, and shake off theire yoake," instead showing faith, patience, and obedience to the hierarchy on earth and in the colony.

Well before the Puritans arrived, Christopher Columbus brought conquest disguised as Christianity to the Americas. One particularly brutal account by Dominican priest Bartolomé de las Casas describes the savagery perpetrated in Florida:

Since 1510 or 1511 three tyrannical adventurers have made their way to these provinces and behaved in much the same way as have their compatriots in other parts of the New World. Two of them already had blood on their hands from campaigns in other parts of the region [Ponce de León and Pánfilo de Narváez], and had clawed their way up to their present commands not on merit but over the dead bodies of their fellow-men....Some three or four years since the above was written, the survivors of this last expedition re-emerged into public view. Their leader did, indeed, meet his end in Florida, but the brutes who were with him were able to give us an account of the dreadful atrocities he and, after his miserable death, they committed among the poor, harmless natives....On their travels, they encountered great settlements whose inhabitants were handsome and intelligent and who lived in well-ordered and structured societies. They murdered many (as is their custom) in order to strike terror into the hearts of these people. They made their lives an utter misery,

[421] John Winthrop, "A Modell of Christian Charity," 1630, https://sites.hks.harvard.edu/fs/phall/03.%20winthrop,%20Christian%20Cha.pdf.

treating them as so many beasts of burden….After the Spaniards had taken their leave, one of the captains, a kinsman of the commander, returned to the town, now basking in the mistaken belief that it was safe from attack, and plundered it, skewering the local leader and king of the entire region on the point of his lance…. Not even the children were spared. It is reported that the butcher-in-chief arranged for a large number of natives in the area and, in particular, one group of over two hundred who had either come from a neighbouring town in response to a summons or had gathered of their own free will, to have their noses, lips and chins sliced from their faces; they were then sent away, in unspeakable agony and all running with blood, to act as walking testimony to the great deeds and holy miracles performed by these dauntless missionaries of the Holy Catholic Faith.[422]

500 years later, Bishop Felipe Estevez of St. Augustine, Florida celebrated the anniversary of Ponce de León's voyage by acknowledging the "great heritage the Spanish brought to 'La Florida,'" not only the art and architecture but also "from the church's vantage point," the greatest of all of Ponce de León's gifts was faith.[423]

Chris Hedges may well be the only Pulitzer Prize journalist to have earned a graduate degree from the Harvard Divinity School; he has also served as a foreign correspondent for the *New York Times* for 15 years and offered this critique in his 2007 bestseller *American Fascists: The Christian Right and the War on America*:

There runs through the fundamentalist belief system a deep

---

[422] Bartolomé de las Casas, *A Short Account of the Destruction of the Indies*, (New York: Penguin, 1992), 102-104.
[423] Margo C. Pope, "Spanish Explorer's 'Greatest Gift' to Florida Was Faith, Says Bishop," Catholic News Service, 11 April 2013.

dread of ambiguity, disorder and chaos. Accordingly, the cult of masculinity keeps all ambiguity, especially sexual ambiguity, in check. It fosters a world of binary opposites: God and man, saved and unsaved, the church and the world, Christianity and secular humanism, male and female. These tidy pairings keep life from slipping back into a complicated nightmare. Reality, thus defined, is made predictable and understandable, something deeply comforting to believers who have had trouble coping with the messiness of human existence. There is, in this 'Christian' worldview, clearly demarcated order and disorder. Behaviors that do not conform— such as homosexuality— are forms of disorder, tools of Satan, and must be abolished. A world that can be predicted and understood, a world that has clear boundaries, can be made rational. It can be managed and controlled. The petrified, binary world of fixed, immutable roles is a world where people, many of them damaged by bouts with failure, despair and their own ambiguities, can bury their chaotic and fragmented personalities and live with the illusion that they are now strong, whole and protected. Those who do not fit, who are not subservient to dominant Christian males, must be proselytized, converted and 'cured' (if they are gay or lesbian) through quack therapy. If they remain recalcitrant they must be silenced. The decline of America is described as the result of the decline of male prowess. This decline has led to weakness and moral decay. It has resulted in a bewildering human and social complexity that, often seen as feminine, is the work of Satan. By submitting to the Christian leader, and to a powerful male God who will destroy those who misbehave, followers avoid dealing with life.[424]

The Koch brothers' political project has cynically ignored their own personal atheism and joined forces with these same fundamentalists, some of whom were rich white business men

---

[424] Chris Hedges, *American Fascists: The Christian Right and the War on America* (New York: Free Press, 2007), Kindle locations 1430-1444.

themselves: Jerry Falwell, Ralph Reed and Tim Phillips, but the Kochs realized that they cannot revolutionize the Republican Party to their benefit without making common cause with the religious right.[425]

In early 2017, a Pulaski County Circuit Judge Wendell Griffen ruled in favor of Merck Pharmaceutical and granted a temporary restraining order before a trial seeking to return the drug manufacturers' products that they alleged Arkansas had obtained fraudulently to use in execution instead of health care. The case, therefore, possibly indirectly complicated the state's plan to execute 11 condemned the same month; the same judge appeared later the same day at a pre-scheduled protest against the death penalty, so Republican lawmakers called for Griffen to be unseated from the bench, and the Arkansas Supreme Court responded by removing Griffen from future capital cases and referred him to the Arkansas Judicial Discipline and Disability Commission to "protect the integrity of the judicial system" and determine whether the judge violated the Code of Conduct.[426] Griffen is an ordained Baptist minister, who explained, sincerely and sensibly, that he is obligated to follow the law as a judge and follow his faith as a clergyman. When the Supreme Court reassigned the Merck case to a new judge, the new judge came to the same conclusion as Griffen had and issued the same temporary restraining order.[427] So, when religion serves hierarchy, the powers that be in the United States embrace it, as Mussolini had in Italy; when religion checks power, as in

---

[425] Nancy MacLean, *Democracy in Chains: The Deep History of the Radical Right's Stealth Plan for America*, (New York: Viking, 2017).

[426] Andrew Demillo, "Arkansas Judge Barred from Execution Cases after Protest," *ABC News*, 17 April 2017.

[427] Amy Goodman, "Exclusive: Meet the Arkansas Judge Who Faces Impeachment for Protesting Against the Death Penalty," *Democracy Now*, 8 May 2017.

Griffen's case, the First Amendment freedom of religion guarantee simply disappears, even for a long-serving judge ruling indirectly on a case that only indirectly jeopardized that state's bloodlust to kill its own people.

Condemned and reprieved Russian novelist and dissident Fyodor Dostoyevsky illustrated his belief that "Compassion is the most important and possibly only law for the whole of human life," in the Christ-like Prince Myshkin, protagonist of *The Idiot*. Early in the novel, Myshkin describes an execution he had witnessed in France, where they cut off people's heads "in the work of an instant," but Myshkin worries that a death "sentence is far more dreadful than a murder committed by a criminal" because the "man who is attacked by robbers at night, in a dark wood, or anywhere, undoubtedly hopes and hopes that he may yet escape until the very moment of his death," whereas "in the case of an execution, that last hope—having which it is so immeasurably less dreadful to die,—is taken away from the wretch and *certainty* substituted," so the official death sentence and its "terrible certainty that he cannot possibly escape death...must be the most dreadful anguish in the world."[428] Yet, the state must have its pound of flesh,[429] and woe be tide to any individual convict, judge, or fictional prince who dare interfere. The truly wise, however, have counseled restraint for millennia, as we read in the Confucian Analects: when Chi K'ang asked Confucius about the morality of "killing the unprincipled for the good of the principled?" Confucius asked "why should you use killing at all?" offering instead: "Let your evinced desires be for what is good, and the people will be good."[430]

In Donald Trump's first college commencement speech as

---

[428] Fyodor Dostoyevsky, *The Idiot*, trans. Eva Martin, (Kindle Edition), 14.
[429] Shakespeare, William. *A Merchant of Venice*, Act IV, Scene I.
[430] Confucius. *Complete Works of Confucius*, (Minerva Classics, 2013), Kindle locations 1200-1203.

president, he addressed graduates of the fundamentalist Christian Liberty University of Jerry Falwell, Jr., who suffered much criticism when he endorsed Trump's candidacy; Trump's speech exhorted the graduates to relish "the opportunity to be an outsider," and embrace that outsider label; being the outsider is fine because "it's the outsiders who change the world and who make a real and lasting difference," concluding with the non-sequitur that in "America, we don't worship government...we worship God."[431] Falwell, ever the political animal himself, had touted Trump as a "successful executive and entrepreneur, a wonderful father and a man who...can lead our country to greatness again."[432]

Many Liberty students, however, rejected Trump, penning an op-ed: "We are Liberty students who are disappointed with President Falwell's endorsement and are tired of being associated with one of the worst presidential candidates in American history....Trump is the antithesis of our values."[433] So, do we thank Sappho, Paine, of perhaps Jesus for the good sense of these sincerely pious Liberty students, who see the danger of merging church and state?[434] And, let's hope that someone shows Falwell and Trump the wisdom of Mathew 22, verse 21: "Render unto Caesar the things that are Caesar's, and unto God the things that are God's." The Liberty University students seem much wiser on this score than President Falwell or President Trump.

---

[431] Callum Borchers, "Trump at Liberty University Commencement: 'In America, We Don't Worship Government; We Worship God.'"
[432] Rebecca Shabad, "Jerry Falwell Jr. Endorses Donald Trump for President," CBS News, 26 January 2016.
[433] Callum Borchers, "Trump at Liberty University Commencement: 'In America, We Don't Worship Government; We Worship God.'"
[434] Emma Green, "Liberty University Students Want to Be Christians—Not Republicans," *The Atlantic*, 26 October 2016.

War

"A standing military...with an overgrown Executive will not...be safe companions to liberty."
  —James Madison

"The bullets pass, Mussolini remains."
  —Benito Mussolini

"Wars are not fought for women's rights, wars are fought for power."
  —Sonali Kolhatkar

"I had been the most tenacious believer in the war," Mussolini explained in his autobiography, bragging about a "citation from [his] superior in these words: 'Benito Mussolini, ever the first in operations of courage and audacity.'"[435] He consistently pursued war in foreign and domestic policy.[436] He saw himself as a warrior and the new Fascist Italy as a warrior nation: "War had left, beyond its inevitable griefs, a deep poetical vein in our national life," claiming that no one "sensed it better, no one seemed more a part of it."[437] He believed that Italy "was in this great historical moment immediately after a victory achieved with untold hardship...in spite of having thrown into the glowing brazier of the conflict men and wealth, was treacherously deceived" by the Treaty of Versailles and had suffered an "awful toll that Italy paid in the Great War--652,000 652,000 dead, 450,000 mutilated, 1,000,000 wounded."[438] Mussolini's rise

---

[435] Mussolini, *My Autobiography*, Kindle locations 478-605.
[436] Stephen Corrado Azzi, "The Historiography of Fascist Foreign Policy," *The Historical Journal* 36, no. 1 (1993): 187, http://www.jstor.org/stable/2639522.
[437] Ibid.

depended primarily on his leadership as a military man and later support by the Italian military of his Fascist regime, which expressly rejected perpetual peace as impractical, if not impossible. Moreover, pacifism was an effete and cowardly renunciation of the duty to the nation, and like Shopenhauer, Mussolini also rejected suicide as a surrender of the intellect, but Shopenhauer's reasoning related to his sense of honor and the duty of individuals never to "use any unjust or unlawful lawful means of getting what we want."[439] Mussolini, on the other hand, considered choosing death a betrayal of ennobled human energies for those who were brave enough to face the alternative of life or death in battle. Evading this ultimate test, therefore, contradicts the doctrine of Fascism. Equally anathema to the spirit of the Fascists were any internationalist organizations, such as President Wilson's League of Nations, because history, according to Mussolini, had proven that such superstructures eventually betray the practical and sentimental ideals of the individual state as member. Ultimately, the Fascist State and each individual Fascist must reject pacifism for a Stoical fighting spirit that is always willing to put everything at risk in order to achieve victory.[440]

In partial contrast, American history from the Revolution shows an ambivalence toward militarism, especially after all of the earth scorched by Sherman in the Civil War. Since World War II, America has also suffered a victory deficit, with many citizens growing weary of such disastrous, bloody, and lost conflicts as Korea, Vietnam, Iraq, and Afghanistan. One troubling response to the ongoing public relations difficulties of sending troops overseas to return in body bags is to privatize

---

[438] Ibid.
[439] Schopenhauer, Arthur. *The Wisdom of Life*. Kindle locations 660-663.
[440] Mussolini, op. cit., Kindle locations 214-227.

operations through the CIA management of secretive mercenaries, such as Erik Prince's now defunct Blackwater Security. After moving to United Arab Emirates to avoid lawsuits and criminal prosecution, Trump advisor Prince continued his global efforts to further such projects as mounting Thrush 510G propeller crop duster airplanes with machine guns, surveillance cameras, and bomb-dropping rigging for service in such theaters as South Sudan to fulfill contracts by Prince's newly named Frontier Services Group.[441] Prince's business plan was to apply strict cost controls on war by circumventing the arms manufacturers and their astronomical price tags for equipment and materiel. Prince bragged to the *Wall Street Journal* that his new endeavor was not patriotic but strictly a money-making venture with Beijing, after being "blowtorched" by U.S. politics.[442] Prince seeks to export Fascism to smaller markets and make a profit while doing so.

Spending on war and weapons, as General Eisenhower informed us, precludes spending on education, health, social programs, or infrastructure:

> Every gun that is made, every warship launched, every rocket fired signifies, in the final sense, a theft from those who hunger and are not fed, those who are cold and are not clothed. This world in arms is not spending money alone. It is spending the sweat of its laborers, the genius of its scientists, the hopes of its children. The cost of one modern heavy bomber is this: a modern brick school in more than 30 cities. It is two electric power plants, each serving a town of 60,000 population. It is two fine, fully-equipped hospitals. It is some fifty miles of concrete pavement. We pay for a single fighter

---

[441] Jeremy Scahill and Mathew Cole. "Echo Papa Exposed," *The Intercept*, 11 April 2016.
[442] David Feith, "Erik Prince: Out of Blackwater and Into China," *Wall Street Journal*, 24 January 2014.

plane with a half million bushels of wheat. We pay for a single destroyer with new homes that could have housed more than 8,000 people. This is, I repeat, the best way of life to be found on the road the world has been taking. This is not a way of life at all, in any true sense. Under the cloud of threatening war, it is humanity hanging from a cross of iron.

The cross is a most bloody one, and the clouds are currently most threatening on the Korean Peninsula, where the United States continually seeks nuclear first-strike capabilities while simultaneously refusing to negotiate a non-aggression-pact or treaty to end the hostilities that began in 1950.[443] The week that Chinese Premier Xi was to visit Mar-a-Lago, former CIA and NSA Director Michael Hayden described North Korea as a "bad toothache" for Beijing, which the former Air Force general suggests solving by aggravating China's pain through deployment of Lockheed's Terminal High Altitude Area Defense (THAAD) system "planted…in South Korea [which would cause] obvious implications for the Chinese because the radar fans go all the way up through Manchuria," but, Hayden counsels, "we should not forego merely because it would upset the Chinese."[444] Upsetting the Chinese should be enough reason to forego the provocation, but returning to General Eisenhower's admonition, the monetary price for deploying the menacing THAAD system is $2 billion,[445] which spending also creates continued support for the Fascist dictatorship inside North Korea to respond and provokes Pyongyang to ignore its own poor and hungry citizenry to instead spend an inordinate percentage of its

---

[443] Benjamin Kang Lim and Ben Blanchard, "North Korea Seeks China Help on Treaty with U.S., or More Tests – Source," Reuters, 8 January 2016.
[444] Nyshka Chandran, "Former CIA Director: THAAD Is a Way Washington Can Pressure China on North Korea," CNBC, 4 April 2017.
[445] David Mosher, "Understanding the Extraordinary Cost of Missile Defense," The Rand Corporation, 2000.

own budget on countering the U.S. threat near its border and renewed sanctions.[446]

China and Russia are responding to provocative U.S. sanctions rhetoric by scheduling first ever joint war games;[447] Russian Vice Admiral Alexander Fedotenkov explained with ambiguity that the "actions of our sailors will be monitored by our numerous neighbors in the region."[448] Deputy Chinese Navy Commander Tian Zhong said that the drills would include air defense, maritime search and rescue, and underway replenishment in an effort to improve strategic military cooperation between China and Russia.[449] Deputy Minister of Defense of the Russian Federation Lieutenant. General Alexander Fomin told Russia's TASS news agency that "the first phase of a large-scale Russian-Chinese navel exercise 'Naval Cooperation 2017' is underway in the Baltic Sea," in which Russian and Chinese "seamen are training together to rebuff threats on high seas," further warning that the "maneuvers will continue in the water areas of the Sea of Okhotsk and the Sea of Japan in autumn." The exercises occur in the context of early June 2017 remarks by United States Secretary of Defense Mattis warning China that the United States "cannot and will not accept unilateral coercive changes to the status quo" and that U.S. military "will continue to fly, sail and operate wherever international law allows and demonstrate resolve through operational presence in the South China Sea and beyond," prompting China's Foreign Ministry Spokesperson Hua

---

[446] Jeremy Laurence and Danbee Moon, "North Korea Spends About a Third of Income on Military," Reuters Canada, 18 January 2011.

[447] Reuters, "US House approves new Russia sanctions, defying Donald Trump," *Telegraph*, 25 July 2017.

[448] "Russia says its Baltic Sea War Games with Chinese Navy not a Threat," Reuters, 26 July 2017.

[449] Prashanth Parameswaran, China, Russia Launch First Military Drills in Baltic Sea, *The Diplomat*, 26 July 2017.

Chunying to respond: "China respects and safeguards all countries' freedom of navigation and overflight in the South China Sea under international law, but definitely opposes certain country's show of force in the South China Sea under the pretext of navigation and overflight freedom, challenging and threatening China's sovereignty and security."[450]

Alexander Hamilton considers the question of imperialism and the United States Commander in Chief in Federalist Paper 69: "The President of the United States would be an officer elected by the people for four years; the king of Great Britain is a perpetual and hereditary prince. The one would be amenable to personal punishment and disgrace; the person of the other is sacred and inviolable." The president "would have a qualified negative upon the acts of the legislative body;" the king "has an absolute negative." The president "would have a right to command the military and naval forces of the nation;" the king, "in addition to this right, possesses that of declaring war, and of raising and regulating fleets." The president "would be an officer elected by the people for four years; the king…is a perpetual and hereditary prince." The president "would be amenable to personal punishment and disgrace;" while the king "is sacred and inviolable."[451] So, the American Constitutional system provides for some checks—if exercised—on authoritarianism, militarism, and imperial expansionism.

The cost for the expansionism and militarism dominates federal discretionary spending of tax dollars, and many of the programs hide outside of the Pentagon. As Director of the Arms and Security Project at the Center for International Policy

---

[450] Sam LaGrone, "China Pushes Back Against SECDEF Mattis 'Irresponsible Remarks' on South China Sea," U.S. Naval Institute, 5 June 2017, https://news.usni.org/2017/06/05/china-pushes-back-secdef-mattis-irresponsible-remarks-south-china-sea.

[451] Alexander Hamilton, *The Federalist Papers*, Number 69 of March 1788.

William D. Hartung details the actual budget for future, present, and past wars that clearly are making us all less, not more, safe:

The Pentagon Budget: Much of the Pentagon budget objectively qualifies as corporate welfare in that many of the weapons systems are not militarily necessary, according to serving generals, and contracts often include waste, if not outright fraud, as outlined in a January 2015 Pentagon report by the Defense Business Board. DBB ultimately recommended $125 million in savings. The Pentagon is always "complaining that they don't have any money," former DBB chairman Robert Stein told the Washington Post, so they "proposed a way to save a ton of money," but Deputy Defense Secretary Robert Work "replied that the recommendations were simply not realistic."[452]

Pentagon Budget: $575 billion

The War Budget: The budget for the wars in Iraq and Afghanistan lies outside of the Pentagon's regular budget. For example, the fiscal year 2017 budget request by the Trump administration continues a questionable practice of including foreign military construction projects under the category of the Overseas Contingency Operations. Some of the biggest projects highlighted by the Taxpayers for Common Sense include "$115 million for a new Army barracks in Cuba....$60 million for a vaguely named 'Supporting Facilities/Utilities' at Muwaffaq Salti Air Base in Jordan."[453]

War Budget: $64.6 Billion

Nuclear Weapons: "It's a $30-billion-a-year organization with about 110,000 employees. Industrial sites across the country.

---

[452] "Pentagon Reportedly Buried Study Exposing $125 Billion in Waste," Fox News, 6 December 2016.
[453] Ryan Alexander, "Off-Budget, Not Out of Mind," *U.S. News & World Report*, 20 June 2017.

Very serious stuff."[454] $20 billion dollars of the Department of Energy budget go to maintaining the 6800 nuclear warheads and funding research in the nuclear weapons laboratories.

Department of Energy: $20 Billion

Other Defense: This catchall category includes "a number of flows of defense-related funding that go to agencies other than the Pentagon," totaling approximately $8 billion per year. "In recent years, about two-thirds of this money has gone to pay for the homeland security activities of the FBI," significantly increasing their annual budget.[455]

Other Defense: $8 Billion

Homeland Security: The Trump White House budget blueprint released early in 2017 stated that the DHS funding "eliminates and reduces unauthorized and under-performing programs," which includes a surprising reduction in the visible response program, but, according to the budget release, the White House "prioritizes DHS law enforcement operations, proposes critical investments in front line border security, and funds continued development of strong cybersecurity" defense.[456]

Homeland Security: $50 Billion

Military Aid: The Trump administration maintains the $7 billion in foreign military aid funneled through the Department of State while cutting global health programs by 25%, cutting international peacekeeping by 50%, cutting educational and

---

[454] Michael Lewis, "Why the Scariest Nuclear Threat May be Coming from Inside the White House," *Vanity Fair*, 26 July 2017.

[455] William D. Hartung, "A Guide to Trump's $1 Trillion Defense Bill," *The Nation*, 25 July 2017.

[456] Mark Berman, "Trump's Dept. of Homeland Security Budget Would Dramatically Cut Counterterrorism Programs, Report Says," *Washington Post*, 13 July 2017.

cultural exchanges by 52%, cutting agricultural, water, and sanitation aid by 45%, but maintaining full funding for NATO.[457]

Military Aid through the State Department: $7 Billion

Intelligence: The 17 agencies mentioned repeatedly by Hillary Clinton in the 2016 presidential campaign include:

1. Office of the Director of National Intelligence
2. Central Intelligence Agency
3. National Security Agency
4. Defense Intelligence Agency
5. Federal Bureau of Investigation
6. Department of State – Bureau of Intelligence and Research
7. Department of Homeland Security – Office of Intelligence and Analysis
8. Drug Enforcement Administration – Office of National Security Intelligence
9. Department of the Treasury – Office of Intelligence and Analysis
10. Department of Energy – Office of Intelligence and Counterintelligence
11. National Geospatial-Intelligence Agency
12. National Reconnaissance Office
13. Air Force Intelligence, Surveillance and Reconnaissance
14. Army Military Intelligence
15. Office of Naval Intelligence
16. Marine Corps Intelligence
17. Coast Guard Intelligence[458]

---

[457] Yeganeh Torbati, "Republicans Push Back Against Trump Plan to Cut Goreign Aid," Reuters, 23 May 2017.

[458] Nina Agrawal, "There's More Than the CIA and FBI: The 17 Agencies that Make Up the U.S. Intelligence Community, *Los Angeles Times*, 17 January 2017.

Intelligence: $70 Billion

Veterans Benefits: The Veterans Administration has requested over $180 billion for the 2018 budget, which is more than three times what it was before the 2001 invasion of Afghanistan. Most of the costs go for health care.[459]

Veterans: $186 billion

Military Retirement: The trust fund set up to cover pensions for military retirees and their survivors doesn't have enough money to pay out all the benefits promised. As a result, it is supplemented annually by an appropriation from the general revenues of the government. That supplement has by now reached roughly $80 billion per year.[460]

Military Retirement: $80 Billion

Defense Share of Interest on the Debt: Interest on the national debt amounts to $500 billion per year, and the Project on Government Oversight calculates the share of the interest on that debt owed due to prior military spending equates to more than $100 billion annually. As Jack Shanahan Fellow at the Project on Government Oversight Dan Grazier commented: "Pumping more money into this system is not the answer. That will only reward continued bad behavior. If President Trump wants to truly rebuild the military, he should actually slash budgets. It would force the Pentagon and Congress to make the difficult choices necessary to produce a more effective" and sustainable military.[461]

---

[459] Molly Redden, "Trans healthcare costs are actually a tiny proportion of the US military budget," *Guardian*, 26 July 2017.

[460] Diane Black, "The Need to Reform Military Compensation," House Budget Committee, 10 December 2013, https://budget.house.gov/hbc-publication/364048/.

[461] Dan Grazier, "President Trump's Pentagon Budget Proposal, More of the Same," Project on Government Oversight, 17 March 2017, http://www.pogo.org/straus/issues/defense-budget/2017/president-trumps-pentagon.html.

Defense Share of the Interest on the Debt: $100 billion

Grand Total: $1.09 Trillion[462]

On April 13, 2017, Commander in Chief Trump spent thousands, if not millions, when he authorized the first ever deployment of the GBU-43/B Massive Ordnance Air Blast (MOAB) over the Achin district of Nangarhar province,[463] not coincidentally the day after the United States military admitted to accidentally killing 18 allies fighting against ISIS in Tabqa.[464] Trump oddly would not take responsibility for directly ordering the 21,600 pound bomb drop, instead evading the question by responding to reporters that "everyone knows what happened....What I do is authorize my military," boasting that "Frankly, that is why they have been so successful lately, if you look at what has happened over the last eight weeks," as compared to Obama's leadership and "what has happened over the last eight years." The show of force met praise from United States Senator from Oklahoma Jim Inhofe, who glowed that the attack "sends a clear message that the United States is committed and determined to defeating ISIS and other terrorist organizations in Afghanistan," which praise United States Senator from South Carolina Lindsey Graham echoed, with the pith of a John Ford Western, on Graham's Twitter feed: "I hope America's adversaries are watching & now understand there's a new sheriff in town."[465]

---

[462] Willian D. Hartung, "What You Actually Spend on the National Security State," *American Conservative*, 26 July 2017.

[463] Lucas Tomlinson, "Watch: MOAB Makes Impact Against ISIS Tunnels in Afghanistan," *FoxNews World*, 14 April 2017.

[464] Molly Hennessy-Fiske, "U.S. military Says Misdirected Airstrike in Northern Syria Killed 18 allied fighters," *Los Angeles Times*, 13 April 2017.

[465] Stephen Collinson, "Trump Carves Out Tough Commander-in-chief Posture," *CNN Politics*, 14 April 2017.

Yet, as United States Congresswoman Jackie Speier criticized, Trump was likely abusing his authority to distract the media and the public from Trump's lackluster performance in his first 100 days: "What concerns [us] most is the fact that what is driving foreign policy is actually our domestic policy [and we are] very concerned that the President is basically taking little responsibility, offering it up to his military when he is the commander in chief"; Speier further explained: "He isn't necessarily front and center evaluating it then speaking to the American people and what his plans are."[466] United States Congressman and Intelligence Committee member Eric Swalwell asked pointedly, "I, too, want to know if the President authorized this—now he doesn't have to authorize everything the military does, but he should certainly be involved when we escalate the weapons used," ending with the poignant observation that "We can't just bomb our way to national security."[467]

Harrington professor of history at the University of Wisconsin-Madison Alfred McCoy predicts dire long and mid-term consequences for the militarized foreign policy of Washington D.C.; his forthcoming book, *In the Shadows of the American Century: The Rise and Decline of US Global Power*, explaining his concerns:

> The American Century, proclaimed so triumphantly at the start of World War II, may already be tattered and fading by 2025 and, except for the finger pointing, could be over by 2030.
>
> For the majority of Americans, the 2020s will likely be remembered as a demoralizing decade of rising prices, stagnant wages, and fading international competitiveness. After years of swelling deficits fed by incessant warfare in

---

[466] Wolf Blitzer, "The Situation Room," *CNN*, 14 April 2017.
[467] Jake Tapper, "The Lead," *CNN*, 14 April 2017.

distant lands, in 2030 the U.S. dollar eventually loses its special status as the world's dominant reserve currency.

Suddenly, there are punitive price increases for American imports ranging from clothing to computers. And the costs for all overseas activity surges as well, making travel for both tourists and troops prohibitive. Unable to pay for swelling deficits by selling now-devalued Treasury notes abroad, Washington is finally forced to slash its bloated military budget. Under pressure at home and abroad, its forces begin to pull back from hundreds of overseas bases to a continental perimeter. Such a desperate move, however, comes too late.

Faced with a fading superpower incapable of paying its bills, China, India, Iran, Russia, and other powers provocatively challenge U.S. dominion over the oceans, space, and cyberspace.[468]

There are—and always have been—alternatives, though. During Roosevelt's buildup to engaging the United States in World War II, Democratic United States Senator Louis Ludlow from Indiana introduced a constitutional amendment that would only allow war to be declared after a national referendum had approved it. The proposed amendment, however, was narrowly defeated by a 209 to 188 margin, but it is encouraging to know that a more peaceful world is possible.[469] A similarly positive 2017 legislative initiative would prohibit any U.S. tax dollars from arming terrorist groups or their associates. Representative and Iraq war veteran Tulsi Gabbard of Hawaii sponsored the original "Stop Arming Terrorists Act," known as H.R. 608, and Senator Rand Paul of Kentucky, introduced a version in the Senate: "One of the unintended consequences of nation-building and open-ended intervention is American funds and weapons benefiting those

---

[468] Alfred McCoy, *In the Shadows of the American Century: The Rise and Decline of US Global Power*, (Chicago, Haymarket, 2017).
[469] David Alexander, *Puzzle Palace*, (Triumvirate Nonfiction, 1983) Kindle locations 611-615.

who hate us," Paul explained.[470] And groups such as Greenpeace urge diplomatic over military solutions: "Importantly the [United Nations] Charter strictly limits the use of force in self-defense to actual occurrences of armed attack," and in the context of anti-Russia hysteria, "the threat or use of nuclear weapons was actually declared illegal by the International Court of Justice in 1996."[471] The people of the United States must demand that the government sees the existential threat of war and the wisdom of peace.

---

[470] Alex Newman, "Congress Considers Bill to 'Stop Arming Terrorists,'" *New American*, 14 March 2017.
[471] "Say No to War and Yes to Peace," Greenpeace, accessed 17 July 2017, http://www.greenpeace.org/international/en/campaigns/peace/say-no-to-war-and-yes-to-peace/.

Politics

"Let the Capitalists do their own fighting, and there will never be another war."
 —Eugene V. Debs

"An election may be considered a childish play, in which the most important part is played by the elected."
 —Benito Mussolini

"The only way to survive is by taking care of one another."
 —Grace Lee Boggs

Toward the end of World War I, Mussolini began expressing his vision of a new politics formed in response to what he saw as the failures of the traditional politics and parties as well as the coming challenges of the modern world.[472] On 23 March 1919, months before the consummation of the Treaty of Versailles, he "laid down the fundamental basis…of the Italian *fasci di combattimento*, the fighting Fascist program" at a meeting in Milan; from the start Mussolini saw politics as combat, and he intended to employ paramilitary to achieve his political aims, as many authoritarian leaders would do after him.[473] He described the meeting as "purely political" in his autobiography and had advertised in the newspaper *Popolo d'Italia* that the event "would have for its object the foundation of a new movement and the establishment of a programme and of methods of action for the success" in the "fight against the forces dissolving victory and the

---

[472] S. J. Woolf, "Mussolini as Revolutionary," *Journal of Contemporary History* 1, no. 2 (1966): 189-192, http://www.jstor.org/stable/259930.
[473] Mussolini, *My Autobiography*, Kindle locations 686-687.

nation."[474] This was revolution "clear and strong, the concept of complete rebellion against the decrepit old state that did not of itself know how to die," but Italy was not ready, and the Fascisti "were beaten" in their first elections in November 1919.[475] In 1921, though, Mussolini finaly won a seat in Parliament, in February of 1922 he proposed "the eventuality of dictatorship,"[476] and by 1923 he had united Nationalism with Fascism and began to "rule Italy for her glory and her good fortune," as he deemed fit, having commanded political and paramilitary forces with "very strict orders" to descend on the capital in the infamous March on Rome that established Mussolini and Fascism as the authoritarians that history associates with them.[477]

Reminiscent of Epicurus, nineteenth century philosopher Jeremy Bentham proposed that "Nature has placed mankind under the governance of two sovereign masters, pain and pleasure," which "govern us in all we do, in all we say, in all we think," to the point that "every effort we can make to throw off our subjection will serve but to demonstrate and confirm it," and though "a man may pretend to abjure their empire…in reality he will remain subject to it all the while."[478] Twentieth century psychologist B. F. Skinner would later create an entire school of behavior modification based on the pleasure/pain dichotomy, which authorities have cited as a legitimation of the ancient carrot and stick routine that combines bribes and threats to manipulate or coerce others in what Skinner simply euphemizes as "positive" and "negative reinforcement."[479] Some parents' groups have

---

[474] Ibid., Kindle locations 690-694.
[475] Ibid,, Kindle locations 816-817.
[476] Farrell, *Mussolini*, 3211-3216.
[477] Mussolini, *My Autobiography*, Kindle locations 1274; 1581.
[478] Philip Stokes, *Philosophy 100 Essential Thinkers,* (Arcturus Publishing, 2012) Kindle locations 1939-1942.
[479] Kevin Wilson, "B.F. Skinner and the Psychology of the Markets." *Seeking Alpha*, 30 November 2016.

raised alarm that the Common Core data mining program in connection with so-called intelligent tutoring systems[480] allow the schools and contractors to collect far too much emotional data on children, ostensibly to help tailor or reinforce their learning but also risking the misuse of the same affective data by unscrupulous agents or commercial interests.[481] Given the secrecy and dishonesty of the surveillance state, it is difficult to know to what level the government might transgress privacy in order to gain control through information, information of an extremely personal nature, practically peering into the mind itself and even corners of the mind that the subjects may not fully access consciously themselves. And if government and commercial entities can collect enough data to understand each person's motivations and predict each person's behavior, the potential for an invisible slavery should concern us. Overfunded political campaigns could easily buy such specific and personal data to tailor propaganda to regions, groups, or even individuals through social media, telling each exactly what each wanted to hear and in exactly the way that is most likely to persuade. The likelihood that any politician would be able to keep such disparate and conflicting promises, however, would be minimal, but the successful candidate, once in office, could use the same data and social media to dupe constituents that the politician had kept promises, or was unable to do so only because of some evil force—one that the politician would courageously volunteer to fight if the constituent would only contribute to the next campaign. In such a scheme, the citizen has virtually no power and even little autonomy, the data miners, propagandists, and

---

[480] Adesope W. Ma, O. O., Nesbit, J. C., & Liu, Q, "Intelligent tutoring systems and learning outcomes: A meta-analysis," *Journal of Educational Psychology, 106* (4), 2014, 901–918.
[481] Diane Kepus, "B. F. Skinner's Wildest Dreams, Common Core, DARPA and Children Robots," *News with Views*, 30 March 2017.

professional politicians having usurped it surreptitiously. As Mussolini described it: "An election may be considered a childish play, in which the most important part is played by the elected."

The recent election in North Carolina of a Democratic governor brought an onslaught of un-democratic and anti-democratic responses from Republicans in the legislature and other political entities, prompting University of North Carolina professor of political science Andrew Reynolds to comment that "If it were a nation state, North Carolina would rank right in the middle of the global league table" as a "deeply flawed, partly free democracy that is only slightly ahead of the failed democracies that constitute much of the developing world."[482] Reynolds' Electoral Integrity Project rated the state a dismal 58 on a scale of 100. Some of the developments leading to the low score include the collaboration of the outgoing Republican Governor Pat McCrory with the Republican legislature to enact sweeping limits on the powers of the incoming Democratic Governor Roy Cooper, in effect stripping the new executive of authority that the former executive exercised, especially in the area of appointing officials to draw electoral maps, which the United States Supreme Court eventually struck down as so clearly racially discriminatory as to be unconstitutional: "The Constitution entrusts states with the job of designing congressional districts," writes Justice Elena Kagan in the majority opinion, "but it also imposes an important constraint: A state may not use race as the predominant factor in drawing district lines…."[483] The Gerrymandering of electoral districts transforms voting into worse than a childish play, the manipulation is at least undemocratic in theory and usually anti-democratic in effect

---

[482] Feliks Garcia, "North Carolina Is No Longer a Democracy, Report Says," *The Independent*, 24 December 2016.
[483] Ariane de Vogue, "Supreme Court Strikes Down North Carolina Congressional District Maps," CNN, 22 May 2016.

since the misconduct leads directly to minority rule in opposition to the majority of the constituency.[484] It is important to recall that both Mussolini and Hitler stood for elections, though their countries operated what were eventually one-party systems; but this is the goal and outcome of all of the unethical Gerrymandering: one-party dominance with the illusion of multi-party representation.[485]

Outgoing Office of Government Ethics Director Walter Shaub complained about the specific ethical transgressions in the first six months of the Trump administration:

> By continuing to hold onto his businesses and effectively advertising them through frequent visits to his properties, our leader creates the appearance of profiting from the presidency. As things stand, we can't know whether policy aims or personal financial interests motivate his decisions as president. Whatever his intentions may be, the resulting uncertainty casts a pall of doubt over governmental decision-making.[486]

Straub went on to argue for greater authority of O.G.E., especially the ability to obtain information from the executive branch, including from the increasingly tyrannical Trump White House.

In mid-July of 2017, Trump appointed hedge fund manager Anthony Scaramucci to become communications director. At a 2011 fund-raising event organized by Scaramucci in Las Vegas, complete with "blinis with caviar; a fennel, grapefruit, and

---

[484] Christopher Ingraham, "This Is the Best Explanation of Gerrymandering You Will Ever See: How to Steal an Election: a Visual Guide," *Washington Post*, 1 March 2015.

[485] William F. B. O'Reilly, "Donald Trump, Benito Mussolini and Adolf Hitler: Is There Any Comparison?" *Newsday*, 1 March 2016.

[486] Walter Shaub, "How to Restore Government Ethics in the Trump Era," *New York Times*, 18 July 2017.

pomegranate salad; cocoa-encrusted beef tenderloin; and blue-cheese panna cotta," billionaire attendee Leon Cooperman hand delivered a letter to Al Gore but addressed to President Obama:

> You should endeavor to rise above the partisan fray and raise the level of discourse to one that is both more civil and more conciliatory.... Capitalism is not the source of our problems, as an economy or as a society, and capitalists are not the scourge that they are too often made out to be. As a group we employ many millions of taxpaying people, pay their salaries, provide them with healthcare coverage, start new companies, found new industries, create new products, fill store shelves at Christmas, and keep the wheels of commerce and progress (and indeed of government, by generating the income whose taxation funds it) moving. To frame the debate as one of rich-and-entitled versus poor-and-dispossessed is to both miss the point and further inflame an already incendiary environment.[487]

Cooperman had earlier compared the 2008 election of Obama to the rise of Hitler. The day after the fundraising event, Scaramucci warned that a "sleeper cell" of hedge fund managers "now have the power, because of *Citizens United*, to aggregate capital into political-action committees and to influence the debate," and since President Obama "has a philosophy of disdain toward wealth creation," he would be their first target.[488] It is an interesting comment to read only a short year after the 2010 United States Supreme Court assessed and predicted the following in the *Citizens United* decision:

---

[487] Chrystia Freeland, "Super-Rich Irony: Why Do Billionaires Feel Victimized by Obama?," *New Yorker*, 8 October 2012.

[488] Jon Schwarz, "Anthony Scaramucci, Trump's New Communications Director, Said Citizenx United Made Possible a "Sleeper Cell of Hedge Fund Managers," *Intercept*, 21 July 2017.

[W]e now conclude that independent expenditures, including those made by corporations, do not give rise to corruption or the appearance of corruption. That speakers may have influence over or access to elected officials does not mean that those officials are corrupt. The appearance of influence or access, furthermore, will not cause the electorate to lose faith in our democracy.

Unfortunately, the majority in the case—all Republican-appointees—could not have been more wrong on both counts, and voters have lost faith in democracy, as dismal voter participation numbers reveal. While Belgium voters participate at an average 87.2%, Sweden 82.6%, and Denmark 80.3%, only 55.7% of eligible voters cast ballots in the 2016 U.S. presidential election, below Obama's first election in 2008.[489] Moreover, a 2014 academic study using aggregate voter turnout from thirty-five democracies demonstrated that "people in systems that control corruption effectively, and have fair judicial processes are more likely to vote" because these "systems that treat people in their day-to-day operations make people feel valued by their political system."[490] And, as Justice Stevens wrote in his 90-page dissent (joined by Bader Ginsberg, Breyer, and Sotomayor), federal prohibitions on corporate expenditures have existed for more than sixty years in order to fulfill a "compelling government interest in the prevention of corruption."[491] Given the billions at stake, the corruption quickly leads to a tyranny of the super rich.

---

[489] Drew DeSilver, "U.S. Trails Most Developed Countries in Voter Turnout," Pew Research 15 May 2017.

[490] Matthew R. Miles, "Turnout as Consent: How Fair Governance Encourages Voter Participation," *Political Research Quarterly* 68, no. 2 (2015): 363, http://www.jstor.org/stable/24371838.

[491] Michael S. Kang, "The End of Campaign Finance law," *Virginia Law Review* 98, no. 1 (2012): 12, http://www.jstor.org/stable/41350237.

Yale University professor of history Timothy Snyder recently published a list of lessons on tyranny from the 20th century, and his bestselling book explains each of the below in more detail:

1. Do not obey in advance.
2. Defend institutions.
3. Beware the one-party state.
4. Take responsibility for the face of the world.
5. Remember professional ethics.
6. Be wary of paramilitaries.
7. Be reflective if you must be armed.
8. Stand out.
9. Be kind to our language.
10. Believe in truth.
11. Investigate.
12. Make eye contact and small talk.
13. Practice corporeal politics.
14. Establish a private life.
15. Contribute to good causes.
16. Learn from peers in other countries.
17. Listen for dangerous words.
18. Be calm when the unthinkable arrives.
19. Be a patriot.
20. Be as courageous as you can.[492]

There is almost no substitute for courage, but we must remember to temper courage with wisdom, and ethics. Walter Shaub recommends the following:

> The White House and agencies lacking inspectors general need investigative oversight, which should be coordinated with O.G.E. The ethics office needs more independence, including authority to communicate directly with Congress on budgetary and legislative matters. Because we can no longer

---

[492] Timothy Snyder. *On Tyranny: Twenty Lessons from the Twentieth Century*, (Crown/Archetype, 2017, Kindle Edition), 8-9.

rely on presidents to comply voluntarily with ethical norms, we need new laws to address their conflicts of interest, their receipt of compensation for the use of their names while in office, nepotism and the release of tax forms. Transparency should be increased through laws mandating creation and release of documents related to divestitures, recusals, waivers and training. Disclosure requirements can be refined and the revolving door tightened.[493]

These changes in the O.G.E. would help to address the current challenge, and importantly, reinforce for all future presidents the importance of setting a strong ethical example from the top. This is no substitute, however, for organizing from the bottom. Anyone eligible to vote must register and vote. We must also fight any efforts to decrease eligibility, instead working to expand eligibility. But democracy only begins on election day. As we saw with the disappointing performance of the Obama presidency, when many voters simply walked away after election day, we must make demands, monitor progress on our demands, and then reward or punish elected representatives according to their performance. Democracy as a spectator sport quickly turns into a tragic sham. Most, if not all, important progressive political advances for the vast majority all began at the grass roots level. The wealthy and powerful minority have continuously sought the favor of the Congress, the President, and the Courts to advance agendas that benefit the wealthy and powerful—almost always at the expense of the vast majority. The only way to counteract this inevitable tendency is to pursue our own agendas with more consistency, tenacity, and imagination.

---

[493] Walter Shaub, "How to Restore Government Ethics in the Trump Era," *New York Times*, 18 July 2017.

Justice

"In the absence of justice, what is sovereignty but organized robbery?"
          —Saint Augustine

"They were looking to me as to a chief whose word was law."
          —Benito Mussolini

"Ours is a justice system that harms people who harm people to show that harming people is wrong."
          —Fania Davis

Mussolini spoke of justice in the law and order terms of how deliberately he executed law enforcement actions, and he credited himself "with the fact" as he described it, that he never "lost [his] calm nor [his] sense of balance and justice."[494] Because of the "serene judgment" that he sought "to summon to guide [his] every act," he "ordered the guilty to be arrested," and his sense of justice included bullying workers: "When the menace of a general strike in the Province of Rome arose," Mussolini "ordered the Florentine legions of the Militia to parade in the streets of the Capital" so as to intimidate the workers by "armed Militia with its war songs" as a "great agent of persuasion," against the free expression and association of workers to withhold their own labor; Mussolini later threatened to "make a litter for the Black Shirts," thus equating the protestors as expendable and even trash.[495] Mussolini referred to this plain authoritarianism as a "new sense of justice, of serious purpose, of

---

[494] Mussolini, *My Autobiography*, Kindle locations 2060-2074.
[495] Ibid.

harmony and" ensuring that "nothing is done against the state, nothing is done outside the state."[496] Once in power and having consolidated power to the point of one party rule, Fascists established the Special Tribunal for the Defense of the State in order to prosecute political crimes, creating a climate in which thousands of "Italians dissented in silence...."[497] A military general chaired the court and defendants enjoyed no right of appeal; in its "sixteen years and five months of existence, the Special Tribunal sentenced the 4596 political offenders who came before it to a total of 27,735 years in prison and handed out forty-two death sentences of which thirty-one were carried out— just under two executions a year."[498]

The American pursuit of justice manifests most dramatically in a carceral state that has grown into a cruel system that ruins lives, separates families, decimates communities, and typically fails to rehabilitate, but does generate billions of dollars of revenue for an industry that regularly imposes torturous conditions and even slavery under the color of law.[499] The glaring diminution of civil rights in the system inspired Supreme Court Justice Sotomayor to write in *Utah v. Strieff* that the 21st century justice system in the United States "says that your body is subject to invasion while courts excuse the violation of your rights. It implies that you are not a citizen of a democracy but the subject of a carceral state, just waiting to be cataloged." Once catalogued, the dehumanization and neglect all too often becomes lethal. Michael Anthony Kerr, a North Carolina inmate suffering

---

[496] Ibid., Kindle locations 2217-2221.
[497] Piero Melograni, "The Cult of the Duce in Mussolini's Italy," *Journal of Contemporary History* 11, no. 4 (1976): 222, http://www.jstor.org/stable/260197.
[498] Farrell, *Mussolini*, Kindle locations 5194-5200.
[499] Marie Gottschalk, "America Needs a Third Reconstruction," *The Atlantic,* 18 September 2015.

from mental illness died of thirst after 35 days of solitary confinement; the autopsy report determined that the prison staff had offered the inmate no treatment for his schizophrenia before he died of dehydration; but the report conspicuously did not list when staff last allowed Kerr food or water while in "the hole," so no one was held accountable for Kerr's cruel death.[500] While those who mistreat or neglect inmates or suspects rarely face consequences, those who attempt to enforce rights of the accused or convicted often face vicious public ridicule and intimidation. Roger Ailes successfully mounted the Willie Horton smear campaign accusing presidential candidate Michael Dukakis as weak on crime, contributing to the victory of George H. W. Bush in 1988.[501] In an even more extreme example, retired Marine Corps Colonel Mitchell Paige called for the hanging of Chief Justice Earl Warren due to Warren's decisions that were so weak on crime that Paige determined that the only explanation possible was that communism had tainted Warren's mind.[502] Capitalism, according to Paige's logic, requires harsh punishment.

In the state of Texas, private prisons so nakedly exert their influence in the legislature that Texas State Representative John Raney admitted to the Associated Press on 1 May 2017 that Geo Group officials wrote legislation that Raney introduced: "I've known the lady who's their lobbyist for a long time.... That's where the legislation came from," Raney confessed; "We don't make things up. People bring things to us and ask us to help."[503] Raney portrays giant corporations such as GEO not as powerful,

---

[500] Associated Press, "N. C. inmate died of thirst after 35 days in solitary," *USA Today*, 26 Sep 2014.

[501] O'Ryan Johnson, "Michael Dukakis on Roger Ailes: 'He Was Not My Favorite Person,' " *Boston Herald*, 19 May 2017.

[502] James Bamford, *Body of Secrets: Anatomy of the Ultra-Secret National Security Agency*, (New York: Knopf Doubleday, 2007, Kindle Edition), 66.

[503] David Dayen, "Private Prison Corporation wrote Texas Bill Extending How Long Immigrant Children Can Be Detained, *The Intercept*, 2 May 2017.

for-profit entities but rather as entities that need government assistance—corporate welfare. Specifically, Raney and GEO's bill would enable Immigrations and Customs Enforcement (ICE) to classify family detention centers as legitimate daycare centers so that ICE could detain families for longer than the current 20 days. GEO Group, under the proposed legislation, could detain families indefinitely, thus increasing revenues at such jails as the Karnes facility that earns over $50 million per year in an industry that secured stock price jumps upon the election of Donald Trump—in stark contrast to plummeting stock prices in August 2016, when Obama's Deputy Attorney General Sally Yates announced that the Department of Justice would end contracts with private prisons because of poor performance, poor cost effectiveness, and poor compliance with civil rights.[504]

The role of the police continues on the path of militarization at the federal, state, and local levels. President Trump requested over $70 billion for the Department of Homeland Security for 2018, notably "$100 million to support 20,258 Border Patrol positions, including recruiting, hiring, and training 500 new Border Patrol agents compared to the FY 2017 Annualized Continuing Resolution funding level."[505] The Border Patrol is the largest single force in the nation and continues to demonstrate an alarming disregard for not only human and constitutional rights but also the very laws that they purport to enforce. Complaints of systematic lawlessness by agents date back over 20 years, many at Border Patrol roving checkpoints within 100 miles of the southern border. The American Civil Liberties Union of Arizona assisted in filing a 2013 complaint, listing the following:

[504] Fredereka Schouten, "Private Prisons Back Trump and Could See Big Payoffs with New Policies," *USA Today*, 23 February 2017.
[505] Department of Homeland Security, "FY 2018 Budget in Brief," DHS.gov.

• On May 21, agents stopped United States citizen Clarisa Christiansen driving home west of Tucson with her 7-year-old daughter and her 5-year-old son. After Christiansen demonstrated that she was a citizen, agents demanded that she leave her car so they could search it. When she asked why the agents stopped her, they refused to answer. "Two other agents approached the car. One pulled out a retractable knife, threatened to cut her out of her seat belt if she didn't get out of the car and took the keys from her ignition," as Christiansen attempted to leave, "she noticed that one of her tires had been punctured, with a long cut along the sidewall."[506]

• On April 15, United States citizen Ernestine Josemaria passed a Border Patrol vehicle on Indian Route 15 about 50 miles north of the border on the Tohono O'odham Reservation. While driving toward Santa Rosa, Arizona, the Border Patrol vehicle tailgated Josemaria into town and pulled her over. The agents yanked Josemaria out of her truck, twisted her arms, handcuffed her, accused her of drug smuggling, and damaged her vehicle as they searched it against her will. Agents forced Josemaria "to wait for an hour for a drug-sniffing dog, which found nothing."[507]

• On March 22, United States citizen Bryan Barrow was returning from a hike at Fort Bowie National Historic Site in southeastern Arizona, and when Barrow "couldn't find his registration and insurance card immediately, the ranger held him and called for a Border Patrol agent and canine," that "searched the vehicle without Barrow's consent, damaging it. Barrow was detained for four hours without food, water or bathroom access"; in response The Border Patrol denied a related claim from Barrow's insurance company, citing

---

[506] Bob Ortega, "Border Patrol Hit with Abuse Complaints," *Arizona Republic*, 9 October 2013.
[507] Ibid.

federal law that "bars recovery for property damaged by CBP employees while the property is under detention in CBP custody."[508]

• In spring 2011, United States citizen Suzanne Aldridge was driving home to Bisbee, Arizona when a "man in plain clothes who did not identify himself pulled her over," and "questioned her aggressively," demanding to search her car, but when she declined, uniformed "Border Patrol agents dragged her out of her car, handcuffed her and pushed her to the ground," without justification or even explanation.

When Christiansen, Barrow and Aldridge filed internal complaints, the Border Patrol ignored them, prompting ACLU lawyer James Duff Lyall to lodge an administrative complaint to the Department of Homeland Security's inspector general and the department's Office of Civil Rights and Civil Liberties, as well as the Department of Justice. "Many people don't understand what their rights are with regard to their interactions with the Border Patrol," and it is obvious that many "Border Patrol agents don't understand the limits of their authority," said Lyall.[509] The abuses continue, however, and the "length of time from receiving an allegation of misconduct to imposing final discipline is far too long," according to an internal Border Patrol report on disciplining agents, with the "average case involving allegations of serious misconduct tak[ing] more than a year and a half from intake to final disposition of discipline."[510]

In another disturbing development of the reactionary and authoritarian tenure of U. S. Attorney General Jefferson Beauregard Sessions, III, the Justice Department reinstated the

---

[508] Ibid.
[509] Ibid.
[510] Gustavo Solis, "Here's What Immigrants Said About Border Patrol Abuse," *Desert Sun*, 15 March 2016.

practice of allowing state and local law enforcement agencies to seize cars, cash, or other property from persons who are only suspected of crimes—before they are convicted or even charged. The department issued new guidelines on the civil asset forfeiture program in mid-July 2017. Deputy Attorney General Rod J. Rosenstein claimed that the move "is not about taking assets from innocent people," but rather "about taking assets that are the proceeds of, or the tools of criminal activity, and primarily drug dealing."[511] But a 2016 study found excessive fraud and abuse in the program in Illinois, where 89 percent of voters responding to an Illinois Policy Institute poll opposed seizures of property from persons not yet convicted of a crime, and in a joint study with the American Civil Liberties Union of Illinois found that authorities seized $319 million worth of property from 2005 to 2015; ACLU attorney Ben Ruddell argued that the "burden of proof needs to be where it belongs — with the government to prove that there was a crime before they can" seize property.[512] The practice raises issues with the Third Amendment, which was intended to prevent the use of the general warrants and property seizures committed by British troops against the colonists during and before the Revolution.[513] The monies from the current seizures go to buying weapons, or "toys," as police vendors refer to them.[514] The revenue source is too tempting, though, and an increasingly unequal distribution of income and wealth creates fear among those at the top, fear that seeks security in over-arming a warrior cop force.[515]

---

[511] Rebecca R. Ruiz, "Justice Dept. Revives Criticized Policy Allowing Assets to Be Seized," *New York Times*, 19 July 2017.

[512] "State: Civil Asset Forfeiture Cost Residents More Than $300M, *Rock River Times*, 11 November 2016.

[513] Radley Balko, "How Did America's Police Become a Military Force on the Streets? Rise of the Warrior Cop," *ABA Journal* 99, no. 7 (2013): 47.

[514] Shane Bauer, "The Making of the Warrior Cop," *Mother Jones*, 23 October 2014.

A related program transfers millions of weapons and related items from the Department of Defense to federal, state, and local law enforcement, exceeding $2 billion in value and including the following:

- 7,091 trucks ($400.9 million); 625 mine-resistant vehicles (421.1 million); 471 helicopters ($158.3 million); 56 airplanes ($271.5 million); and 329 armored trucks and cars ($21.3 million);

- 83,122 M16/M14 rifles (5.56mm and 7.62mm) ($31.2 million); 8,198 pistols (.38 and .45 caliber) ($491,769); and 1,385 riot 12-guage shotguns ($137,265);

- 18,299 night-vision sights, sniper scopes, binoculars, goggles, infrared and image magnifiers ($98.5 million); 5,518 infrared, articulated, panoramic and laser telescopes ($5.5 million);

- 866 mine detecting sets, marking kits, and probes ($3.3 million); 57 grenade launchers ($41,040);

- 5,638 bayonets ($307,769) and 36 swords and scabbards.

- In Florida, the state highway patrol received 1,815 M16/M14 rifles (5.56mm and 7.62mm), plus six military-armored vehicles, three Mine Resistant Vehicles and three Complete Combat/Assault/Tactical Wheeled Vehicles.

- In California, 18,794 DOD transactions transferring weaponry including nearly 7,500 trades involving M16/M14 rifles. The University of California at Berkley accepted the delivery of 14 M16 rifles. Yet that paled in comparison to the

---

[515] Radley Balko, "Rise of the Warrior Cop," *Wall Street Journal*, 7 August 2013.

1,105 M16/M14 rifles (5.56mm and 7.62mm) and two mine-resistant vehicles acquired by the Los Angeles County Sheriff.

• In Washington, D.C., the Metropolitan Police procured 500 M16 rifles – which is half of what the entire state of New Jersey received in rifles. The DC Metro Transit police have also followed a federal procurement process to obtain 134.5 lbs. of C4, TNT, potassium chlorate, semtex (plastic explosive), and other explosives over the next nine years.

• Many small towns across America received military weapons. Granite City, IL (pop. 29,375) received 25 M16 and M14 rifles (5.56mm and 7.62mm), plus a military-armored truck and a robot for 'explosive ordinance disposal.' Lacon, IL (pop. 1,853) received six .45 and .38 special pistols, five M16/M14 (5.56mm and 7.63mm), and a 12-gage 'riot' shotgun.[516]

Perhaps most bizarre are the 5,638 bayonets (knives attached to the end of rifles) that went to Customs and Border Protection, Alcohol Tobacco and Firearms, Drug Enforcement Agency, and the FBI. Why would law enforcement stab or slice suspects in a democracy? Fortunately, President Obama signed an executive order prohibiting the transfer of bayonets and grenade launchers after 2015. The ACLU announced their support of Obama's ban: "Grenade launchers, high-caliber weapons, armored vehicles…never belonged in our neighborhoods."[517]

When government authorities fail or refuse to hold their officials, agents, employees, or contractors accountable, civil

---

[516] Adam Andrzejewski, "War Weapons for America's Police Departments: New Data Shows Feds Transfer $2.2B in Military Gear," *Forbes*, 10 May 2016.

[517] Adam Shaw, "Outrage as Military Vehicles, Equipment Taken from Officers in Wake of Obama Order," Fox News, 23 November 2015.

society and activists must engage, as Cynthia Pompa of the New Mexico Regional Center for Border Rights did in a 2016 statement: "Every day, thousands of students, workers and tourists legally cross our ports of entry to do business or visit family." Pompa correctly concluded that when "unprofessional or downright cruel CBP officers humiliate, discriminate and physical or verbally abuse them, their mistreatment and lack of accountability offends American values of equality and justice."[518] The next year, thousands of ordinary citizens bodily protested Trump's related travel ban; many actions occurring at international airports in large coastal cities, but others surprised the heartland, such as protestors chanting "No hate, no fear, refugees are welcome here" outside the Ohio statehouse.[519] And former Seattle Chief of Police Norm Stamper recommends the following three major steps to institute meaningful reform:

> *The first* is to end this nation's destructive, immoral drug war. When Richard Nixon famously proclaimed drug abuse 'public enemy number one' and declared all-out war on 'drugs,' he was in truth declaring war against his own people—most notably young people, poor people, and people of color. Since his announcement in 1971, we have spent $1.3 trillion prosecuting the drug war; incarcerated tens of millions of nonviolent drug offenders, breaking up families and destroying individual lives in the process; and transformed the nation's domestic peacekeepers into a hostile, occupational force on the streets of America's neighborhoods. And what do we have to show for it? Drugs are more readily available, at lower prices and higher levels of potency than

---

[518] Clark Mindock, "Border Patrol Abuse 2016: Agents Detained, Harassed Visa Holders, US Citizen, ACLU Alleges," *International Business Times*, 18 May 2016.
[519] Emanuella Grinberg and Eliott C. McLaughlin, "Travel Ban Protests Stretch into Third Day from US to UK," CNN, 31 January 2017.

ever before. Use the billions of dollars saved for prevention, education, treatment.

Second, let's redefine community policing and reject any definition that does not carve out a powerful, sanctioned leadership role for a city or a county's citizens. How about a 51-49 partnership with the community as senior partner? Citizens should be involved in all aspects of police operations, from hiring decisions to oversight of police misconduct and lethal-force investigations.

Third, however repellent to devotees of 'home rule,' we must establish a meaningful and muscular role for the federal government in local policing. There are roughly 18,000 federal, state, and local law enforcement agencies—but only one constitution. The U.S. Constitution is binding on every cop and every department in the country. Yet, from huge urban centers to tiny rural communities, we continue to witness systemic police abuses of the most basic law of the land.

The Department of Justice, working with local communities, must undertake a comprehensive project to (a) formulate national standards of performance and conduct in all areas of procedural justice, such as stop and frisk, search and seizure, laws of arrest, forfeited assets and use of force; (b) certify all law enforcement officers and agencies (including campus police) that meet these standards; and (c) decertify, for cause, any officer or agency that fails to play by the rules.

The problems of policing are national in scope, constitutional in nature. A combination of grassroots activism and congressional action, aided by reform-minded police executives, sympathetic rank-and-file officers, and local officials, can bring about both true community policing and robust police accountability.[520]

---

[520] Norm Stamper, "Former Chief Norm Stamper: Police Forces Belong to the People," *Time*, 11 July 2016.

Eric Michael Moberg

We must insists that our law enforcement respect rule of law and abandon shock and awe tactics of a Nixonian-Trumpian law and order mentality that turns police away from protecting and serving and into occupying forces that intimidate and oppress.

Education

"It is safer to have the whole people respectably enlightened than a few in a high state of science and the many in ignorance."
　—Thomas Jefferson

"The Fascist State makes its action felt throughout the length and breadth of the country by means of its corporative, social, and educational institutions...."
　—Benito Mussolini

"I'm not a numbers person."
　—Betsy DeVos

Mussolini served as a school teacher before his war service and journalism career, and he decided that many in the middle class did not show the public schools enough respect to the institutions. He drafted a four point doctrine that began with rejecting both "the democratic concept which considered a state school as an institution for every one-a basket into which treasure and waste were piled together," and the "purely utilitarian aims, such as a degree or a perfunctory passing to promotions."[521] His second point was to ensure that students at the independent and Catholic schools should "find themselves under equal conditions when taking the state examinations, before committees appointed by the government," such as "the regime of independent schools analogous to those of England." This control over private and religious school testing of the youth in Italy was consistent with the Fascist dictum that everything should be within the state and nothing outside the state. Third, he further emphasized that the Fascist State should watch "over the independent schools" in

---

[521] Mussolini. *My Autobiography*, Kindle locations 2598-2605.

order to promote "a rivalry between independent and state schools" that would serve to raise "the cultural level and the general atmosphere of all schools."[522] The fourth aim was to create more rigor, especially by instituting both admission and graduation by examination. He sought to replace "the disorder and the easy-going ways of the old democratic schools," with a higher "standard of scholarship" leading to a "broad humanistic culture," as well as "technical institutes of higher specialization," and scientific lyceums, teachers' institutes, and classical lyceums focusing on Latin and Roman history.[523] Mussolini anticipated, therefore, not only the zero tolerance mentality of suspending and expelling undesirable students but also the standardized testing and Common Core movements in the United States decades later, and his first Minister of Education, Giovanni Gentile, required that Italian teachers emphasize a "concentration of attention and admiration on Italian literature, Italian geography, history, heroes,"[524] and political tradition, as we see in the 2016 Republican Party platform promoting U.S. nationalism.[525]

The Federalist Papers mention education only once and only indirectly in a discussion of what should be the qualifications of a senator: "The qualifications proposed for senators…must have been a citizen nine years…ought to be exercised by none who are not thoroughly weaned from the prepossessions and habits incident to foreign birth and education."[526] The closest the Constitution comes to even mentioning education lies in the

---

[522] Ibid., Kindle locations 2606-2611.
[523] Ibid., Kindle locations 2611-2617.
[524] A. J. Watt, "Giovanni Gentile: Mussolini's Favourite Educational Philosopher," *The Journal of Educational Thought* (JET) / *Revue De La Pensée Éducative* 15, no. 2 (1981): 129, http://www.jstor.org/stable/23768500.
[525] John Barrasso, Mary Fallin, and Virginia Foxx, "Education: A Chance for Every Child," *Republican Platform 2016*, 33.
[526] Alexander Hamilton, John Jay, and James Madison, *The Federalist Papers*, (Kindle, 2011), 99.

"general welfare" clause of the preamble, echoed in Article one, Section eight: "The Congress shall have Power To lay and collect Taxes, Duties, Imposts and Excises, to pay the Debts and provide for the common Defence and general Welfare of the United States...." Thomas Jefferson did, however, comment at the time on the importance of the issue: "Educate and inform the whole mass of the people, enable them to see that it is their interest to preserve peace and order," because the people are "the only sure reliance for the preservation of our liberty," and indeed "the will of the majority should prevail."[527] Jefferson continued to pursue the issue by proposing public education bills in 1779 and 1796, achieving only limited success in the Virginia Legislature, the establishment of elementary schools—subject to the discretion and financing of each county itself.[528] Jefferson correctly complained that the compromise "would throw on wealth the education of the poor" and since "the more wealthy class were unwilling to incur that burden...it was not suffered to commence in a single county."[529] Jefferson also made an early argument for meritocracy in an 1813 letter to John Adams: "I agree with you that there is a natural aristocracy among men," that should replace the artificial aristocracy "founded on wealth and birth without either virtue or talents."[530] But it was not until 1818 that the Virginia Legislature finally passed the law to establish the University of Virginia as the first public university in the United

[527] Thomas Jefferson, "From Thomas Jefferson to Uriah Forrest, with Enclosure, 31 December 1787, National Archives, accessed 12 July 2017, http://founders.archives.gov/documents/Jefferson/01-12-02-0490.

[528] "Education as the Keystone to the New Democracy," National Park Service, accessed 12 July 2017, https://www.nps.gov/nr/twhp/wwwlps/lessons/92uva/92facts1.htm.

[529] Thomas Jefferson, Andrew A Lipscomb, Albert Ellery Bergh, "The Writings of Thomas Jefferson 1," (Washington, D.C.: Thomas Jefferson Memorial Association of the United States, 1903-04), 70.

[530] Ibid., 13, 399.

States, consistent with Jefferson's vision "to create a better institution of higher learning, one that would prepare America's citizens to lead and govern the new nation," an institution with a "cross-disciplinary exchange between the sciences and humanities, history and chemistry, and students and professors," in a milieu that "would encourage the academic enterprise to advance knowledge, train leaders and break through traditional boundaries."[531]

The struggle for universal quality public education has continued through the decades into the next two centuries with desegregation cases such as *Brown v. Board of Education* and remain in the 21st century with the efforts to defund free and open public education and transfer tax dollars instead to charter, private, and parochial schools, with no evidence of the promised improved student achievement.[532] One can only wonder how Jefferson would respond to the testimony of voucher and charter proponent Betsy DeVos at her 2017 Senate confirmation hearings to serve as Secretary of Education; her performance was so underwhelming that Republican Senators Susan Collins of Maine and Lisa Murkowski of Alaska publicly denounced DeVos' lack of understanding of public school issues. Billionaire education activist Eli Broad wrote to senators that with the clearly unqualified "Betsy DeVos at the helm of the U.S. Department of Education, much of the good work that has been accomplished to improve public education for all of America's children could be undone,"[533] mainly through unregulated expansion of charter

---

[531] "Our Endless Pursuit," University of Virginia, accessed 12 July 2017, http://www.virginia.edu/overview.

[532] Brian Gill, P. Mike Timpane, Karen E. Ross, Dominic J. Brewer, Kevin Booker "Rhetoric Versus Reality: What We Know and What We Need to Know About Vouchers and Charter Schools," Rand, 2007, http://www.rand.org/pubs/monograph_reports/MR1118-1.html.

[533] Emma Brown, "Eli Broad, Billionaire Philanthropist and Charter School Backer, Urges Senators to Oppose DeVos," *Washington Post*, 1 February

schools. Senator Collins took to the senate floor to decry DeVos' focus on charter schools and vouchers that "raises the question about whether or not she fully appreciates that the secretary of Education's primary focus must be on helping states and communities … strengthen our public schools," and Senator Murkowski reported thousands of calls from voters expressing concern about DeVos and the worry that "DeVos will force vouchers on Alaska," leading Murkowski to pronounce that "Mrs. DeVos has much to learn about our nation's public schools, how they work and the challenges they face."[534]

In addition to the concern related to shifting tax dollars away from neighborhood public schools arises the issue of what would the curriculum be at a DeVos style unregulated charter school. Ingham County Circuit Court Judge William Collette ruled the original Michigan charter school law unconstitutional in 1994 based on the well-founded concern that the state could not ensure that charter schools would not violate the principle of separation of church and state: "They are not accountable to anyone," said lawyer for the plaintiffs William F. Young; "That lack of accountability troubled the judge."[535]

A thorough investigation by *Detroit Free Press* revealed many other troubling aspects of the private takeover of public schools, including statutes and regulations that DeVos had lobbied to enact. The numbers that are most telling involve where the money goes: "based on 2012-13 data found traditional schools spend an average of $6,985 per student in the classroom, and charter schools spend $4,893. At traditional schools, administration costs an average of $1,090 per student, compared

---

2017.

[534] Evan Halper, "Confirmation of Betsy DeVos as Secretary of Education in Peril as Two GOP Senators Defect," *Los Angeles Times*, 1 February 2017.

[535] Drew Lindsay, "Mich. Judge Strikes Down Charter Law," *Education Week*, 9 November 1994.

with $1,894 in charter schools."[536] While libertarians and conservatives consistently tout the efficiency of business over government management,[537] the Michigan numbers show the opposite, and the more money spent on management, the less is available for teacher salaries and classroom materials. With Michigan taxpayers funding charter schools at the rate of $1 billion a year and serving over 140,000 students, the state allows alarming leeway and secrecy to the charter schools, many of which operate for-profit; perhaps most alarming is the fact that Michigan sets no standards whatever for who can operate a charter school, how to oversee the institutions, or how to close a failing charter.[538] "People should get a fair return on their investment," according to former state schools Superintendent Tom Watkins, who is himself a longtime charter advocate, but who argues for higher standards: "in a number of cases, people are making a boatload of money, and the kids aren't getting educated."[539] To the corporate-fascist powers that be, making boatloads of money is ultra-American while they enact Mussolini's principle of separating "treasure" into the exclusive private schools and the "trash" into defunded public schools or unregulated charter schools, and they see Jefferson's quest for enlightenment as a counterproductive project that only serves to agitate the masses, who are expected to labor and consume but not to think.

---

[536] Jennifer Dixon, "Michigan Spends $1B on Charter Schools but Fails to Hold Them Accountable," *Detroit Free Press*, 22 June 2014.

[537] Dinyar Godrej, "Myth 5: The private sector is more efficient than the public sector," *New Internationalist*, 1 December 2015, https://newint.org/features/2015/12/01/private-public-sector.

[538] Allie Gross, "Betsy DeVos's Accountability Problem," *Atlantic,* 13 January 2017.

[539] Dixon, "Michigan Spends $1B on Charter Schools but Fails to Hold Them Accountable."

Many 21st century education commentators argue for a return to the vision of Jefferson, especially at the college level. Cultural critic Andrew Delbanco laments the economic necessity of more and more students to obtain practical professional credentials, eschewing the liberal arts tradition that serves as "an exploratory time for students to discover their passions and test ideas and values with the help of teachers and peers."[540] Delbanco worries that such an education has become a luxury available only to the privileged children of the wealthy. Trained aerospace engineer Alan Collinge exposed the predatory practices of the $85-billion college loan industry that has burgeoned since enabling federal legislation beginning during the Clinton presidency. The average debt for a graduate student in the United States is over $40,000 while tuition has increased at more than twice the rate of inflation.[541] Economist Nancy Folbre describes her frustrations as a public university professor trying to teach amid rising student debt burdens, tuition hikes, and budget cuts. Folbre further explains the importance of quality and affordable public higher education to the democracy, and she chronicles the growing development of coalitions pursuing strategies to simplify financial aid, improve quality, and increase access for all.[542] Reformers such as Diane Ravitch also urge a reduction in standardized testing and an emphasis on critical thinking; and presidential candidate Jill Stein championed the following education reforms:

---

[540] Andrew Delbanco, *College: What it Was, Is, and Should Be*, (Princeton, New Jersey: Princeton University Press, 2012).

[541] Alan Collinge, *The Student Loan Scam: The Most Oppressive Debt in U.S. History and How We Can Fight Back*, (New York: Beacon Press, 2009).

[542] Nancy Folbre, *Saving State U: Fixing Public Higher Education*, (New York: The New Press, 2010).

Student debt: We can forgive the crushing student debt burden and liberate an entire generation of young people who are being turned into indentured servants. We have the power to abolish student debt and provide education for all as a right.

Charter schools: We've seen a common pattern with the education agenda pushed by Wall Street and standardized test corporations: high-stakes testing sets up public schools to fail, paving the way for the takeover of education by charter schools with their profits subsidized by taxpayer dollars.

Free education: We can provide tuition-free education from pre-kindergarten through college - an investment in our future that will pay off enormously.

Teacher evaluations: Evaluate teacher performance through assessments by fellow professionals. Do not rely on high-stakes tests that reflect economic status of the community, and punish teachers working in low-income communities of color.

Standardized testing: We must end the high stakes testing that is harmful especially to challenged learners, and used to justify closing and privatizing schools, and to dis-empower teachers and unions.

Federal funding: Increase federal funding of public schools to equalize public-school funding.

Teachers: It's time to provide small classrooms, to pay our teachers well, to honor their unions, and to teach to the whole student for lifetime learning – with enriched with arts, music and recreation, and nurture the independent, creative minds and spirits that Democracy depends on.

Discipline: Use restorative justice to address conflicts before they occur, and involve students in the process.

Department of Education: Use Department of Education powers to offer grants and funding to encourage metropolitan desegregation plans based on socio-economically balanced schools.[543]

The education of all is crucial not only to the competitiveness of workers and industry in the global economy but also to the ability of citizens and voters to participate, question, and dissent in a vibrant democracy.

---

[543] Maureen Sullivan, "Jill Stein on Education: 10 Things the Presidential Candidate Wants You to Know," *Forbes*, 31 August 2016.

The Individual

"I say whatever one loves best is the most beautiful thing."
  —Sappho

"If liberalism spells individualism, Fascism spells government."
  —Benito Mussolini

"The Government says the terrorists hate our freedom and they want to take it, so the government is gonna take it first, that way, when the terrorists show up, it's already gone."
  —Jimmy Dore

Mussolini subordinates the individual to the Fascist State, which is "based on millions of individuals who recognize its authority, feel its action, and are ready to serve its ends."[544] He claimed that the Fascist State was a unique, strong and organic body that was not reactionary, not revolutionary. According to Mussolini's autobiography: "The individual in the Fascist State is not annulled but rather multiplied, just in the same way that a soldier in a regiment is not diminished but rather increased by the number of his comrades."[545] Mussolini's ideal Fascist was both modern but also classic, exemplifying *"romanità"*: Roman-ness.[546] He went on to argue that while the "Fascist State organizes the nation," it allows a "sufficient margin of liberty to the individual" but qualified that the individual "is deprived of all useless and possibly harmful freedom," clarifying that "the deciding power in this question cannot be the individual, but the State alone."[547]

---

[544] Mussolini, *The Doctrine of Fascism*.
[545] Mussolini, *My Autobiography*, Kindle locations 2963-2981.
[546] Jan Nelis, "Constructing Fascist Identity: Benito Mussolini and the Myth of 'Romanità,'" *The Classical World* 100, no. 4 (2007): 393.

This is a strange sort of "freedom," one that the ostensibly free individual is not respected enough to determine or pursue individually, unless of course the individual agrees entirely with the type of freedom allowed by the deciding power itself: the Fascist State alone.

In the United States, however, individuals are respectable to the extent that they can "present themselves as wholly original, self-contained, and independent intelligences," and we measure their success in terms of marketable accomplishments and accumulation of wealth and prestige.[548] Their contribution to society lies in pursuing their own interest, even if they do so with all the selfishness of Gordon, "greed is good," Gekko.[549] And, on the other end of the socioeconomic status ladder, individuals in American Corporate-Fascism are free to fail economically, free to starve, free to be homeless, and free to die due to lack of health care because government is not supposed to pick winners and losers, as Trump advisor Peter Thiel celebrates in his book, *Zero to One: Notes on Startups, or How to Build the Future*.[550]

Civil rights leader Frederick Douglass, though, espoused a distinct view of the individual: "Conscience is, to the individual soul, and to society, what the law of gravitation is to the universe," because the thoughtful individual "holds society together…the basis of all trust and confidence…the pillar of all

---

[547] Ibid.

[548] Anne Carolyn Klein, quoted in Susan Dunston "In the 'Light Out of the East': Emerson on Self, Subjectivity, and Creativity,"
Source: *The Journal of Speculative Philosophy* 26, No. 1 (2012), 25-42,
http://www.jstor.org/stable/10.5325/jspecphil.26.1.0025.

[549] Max Presnell, "V'Landys Sticks to His Guns in Fight Against Southerners," *Syndey Morning Herald*, 21 Juley 2017.

[550] Gordon Campbell, "On Peter Thiel's Bad Attitude Problem,"
Scoop Independent News, 3 July 2017,
http://www.scoop.co.nz/stories/HL1707/S00002/gordon-campbell-on-peter-thiels-bad-attitude-problem.htm.

moral rectitude," for without the courage of individuals, "suspicion would take the place of trust; vice would be more than a match for virtue; men would prey upon each other, like the wild beasts of the desert; and earth would become a hell."[551] Douglass anticipated the suspicion and predation of Fascism with its beastly and hellish disregard for the sanctity and dignity of each individual. The conscience of each individual to Douglass is the very basis of decent society, but to Mussolini any individual morality or philosophy that ventures outside of the doctrine of the state is dangerous, if not treasonous, including disagreement with Mussolini on a political matter such as the status of Dalmatia after the war.[552]

While the individual in the United States has enjoyed many freedoms, notwithstanding sexism and racism, American Corporate-Fascism often serves to undermine the enjoyment of those freedoms in the machinations of a capitalism that alienates individuals from their communities, their coworkers, their families, and even their own work in "something approaching a Kafkaesque world, insignificant and at the mercy of unchallengeable and invisible forces … a world of make-believe, a gigantic hoax."[553] The modern American worker daily "meets a denial that the individual is genuinely significant," writes George Charles Roche, "on every hand he is confronted with vast constitutional amassments that seem beyond his control and his comprehension," in an "Age of Bewilderment."[554] As Studs

---

[551] Frederick Douglass, *The Most Complete Collection of Written Works & Speeches by Frederick Douglass*, (Northpointe Classics, 2011), Kindle locations 15878-15881.
[552] Mussolini, *My Autobiography*, Kindle locations 630-636.
[553] Hans Morgenthau, "Reflections on the End of the Republic," *New York Review of Books*, September 24, 1970, http://www.nybooks.com/articles/1970/09/24/reflections-on-the-end-of-the-republic/.
[554] George Charles Roche quoted in Bertram Gross, *Friendly Fascism: The*

Terkel chronicled from interviews with actual workers: "'I'm a machine,' says the spot welder. 'I'm caged,' says the bank teller, and echoes the bank clerk. 'I'm a mule,' says the steelworker. 'A monkey can do what I do,' says the receptionist."[555] And the bewilderment transcends the work place: "Throughout the middle and lower classes, people learn that there are mysterious powers that bring about higher taxes, higher prices, diminished job opportunities, and abundant shortages," while countless "promises of politicians— whether liberal, conservative, or radical— to do something are discounted," as the growing numbers "of the so-called 'silent majority' feel isolated, self-estranged, and powerless— out of touch with themselves, with most other people, with the dominant institutions of society."[556] A 1973 report by the Secretary of Health, Education, and Welfare found that many Americans had become "alienated from their society, aggressive against people unlike themselves, distrusting of others and harboring an inadequate sense of personal or political efficacy."[557]

In 1977, Walter J. Krueckel published a list of ten warning signs of Fascist traits inside the individual:

1. Rigid adherence to a set of primarily conventional and pre-defined values without question, resulting in moralism.
2. Submission to idealized authority.

New Face of Power in America, (New York: Open Road Media, 2016), 108.

[555] Studs Terkel, *The Studs Terkel Reader: My American Century*, (New York: The New Press, 2011), 302.

[556] Bertram Gross, *Friendly Fascism: The New Face of Power in America*, 108.

[557] Secretary of Health, Education, and Welfare, *Work in America: Report of a Special Task Force to the Secretary of Health, Education, and Welfare*, (Washington D.C.: U. S. Government Printing Office, 1973), 25.

3. Over-competitiveness and the striving for power over others; preoccupation with strong/weak, winner/looser, leader/follower dimensions.

4. Fear of independent thinking; stereotyping and a disposition to think in rigid categories.

5. Mystical escapism; fatalism and cynicism.

6. Fear of others and the need for 'enemies.'

7. Projection upon scapegoats, inability to accept failure.

8. Acceptance of a purely material definition of 'success'; classism.

9. Irrational and unconditional defense of attachment to one's family, church or state; 'my country - right or wrong.'

10. Patriarchal sex-role identification.[558]

It is frightening to compare the above list to the recent Republican Party platform and the speeches of their standard-bearing candidates. The published 2016 Republican Party platform begins with the declaration of moral superiority of the United States, offering a vague justification for the plainly nationalistic assertion:

We believe in American exceptionalism.
We believe the United States of America is unlike any other nation on earth.

---

[558] Walter J. Krueckl, *Understanding The Roots Of Fascism: A Study Of The Sources Of Fascism Both Within Ourselves And Society*, (Vancouver: Grove Street Publishing), 42.

> We believe America is exceptional because of our historic
> role — first as refuge, then as defender, and now as exemplar
> of liberty for the world to see.[559]

Under the heading of "Defending Marriage Against and Activist
Judiciary," the platform proclaims that "Traditional marriage and
family, based on marriage between one man and one woman, is
the foundation for a free society and has for millennia been
entrusted with rearing children and instilling cultural values."[560]
Those with other relationships do not belong in the Republican
free society, especially not raising children or establishing values
of our culture. At work, instead of seeking to increase benefits
for individual private sector workers to the level of federal
workers, the platform does the opposite: "The federal workforce
is larger and more highly paid than ever…triple the average non-
cash compensation of the average worker in the private sector,"
and since federal "employees receive extraordinary pension
benefits and vacation time wildly out of line with those of the
private sector, Republicans "urge Congress to bring federal
compensation and benefits in line with the standards of most
American employees," that is by reducing them in a race to the
bottom.[561] Under the heading of "We the People," they claim to
be "the party of the Declaration of Independence and the
Constitution," though the Republican Party did not exist until
nearly 100 years later. More disturbing is the fact that they
ignore the First Amendment prohibition of establishment of
religion clause and mention "God" six times in discussing the

---

[559] John Barasso, Mary Fallin, and Virginia Foxx, *Republican Platform 2016*,
GOP, https://prod-cdn-
static.gop.com/media/documents/DRAFT_12_FINAL[1]-
ben_1468872234.pdf.
[560] Ibid., 11.
[561] Ibid., 8.

founding documents, though the Constitution does not mention the word even once and the Declaration refers only once to "Nature's God."

> We are the party of the Declaration of Independence and the Constitution. The Declaration sets forth the fundamental precepts of American government: That God bestows certain inalienable rights on every individual, thus producing human equality; that government exists first and foremost to protect those inalienable rights; that man-made law must be consistent with God-given, natural rights; and that if God-given, natural, inalienable rights come in conflict with government, court, or human-granted rights, God-given, natural, inalienable rights always prevail; that there is a moral law recognized as "the Laws of Nature and of Nature's God"; and that American government is to operate with the consent of the governed. We are also the party of the Constitution, the greatest political document ever written. It is the solemn compact built upon principles of the Declaration that enshrines our God-given individual rights and ensures that all Americans stand equal before the law, defines the purposes and limits of government, and is the blueprint for ordered liberty that makes the United States the world's freest and most prosperous nation.[562]

Their claim that United States is the freest nation in the world is simply not consistent with their own authoritarian policies and candidates, not to mention the hypocrisy of calling themselves pro-life while the aggressively support capital punishment:

> The constitutionality of the death penalty is firmly settled by its explicit mention in the Fifth Amendment. With the murder rate soaring in our great cities, we condemn the Supreme

---

[562] Ibid., 9.

Court's erosion of the right of the people to enact capital punishment in their states.[563]

All of the 2016 GOP presidential hopefuls supported the death penalty or left it to the states,[564] many in the party continue to reject the LGBQT movement, and Senator Ted Cruz took the extraordinary position of urging states to "ignore" a United States Supreme Court ruling recognizing gay marriage.[565] The GOP continues to urge party members to "just trust" leadership while they increasingly conduct public business in private, assuring followers that Senator McConell and five other white men are ideal leaders who know what is best for the country.[566] Trump advisor Steven Miller publicly asserted presidential supremacy over the other branches of government on the controversial Muslim ban, though not a single of several courts has agreed.[567] Stereotyping of others transcends race and gender to include bashing of political opponents as weak, elitist, insane, or even treasonous.[568] Ambassador to the United Nations Nicky Haley warned the Security Council that the United States might take "considerable military actions" against North Korea if the other

---

[563] Ibid., 39.

[564] Thomas Kaplan and Wilson Andrews, "Presidential Candidates on the Death Penalty," *New York Times*, 11 November 2015, https://www.nytimes.com/interactive/2015/11/11/us/elections/presidential-candidates-on-the-death-penalty.html.

[565] Adam B. Lerner "Ted Cruz: States Should Ignore Gay-Marriage Ruling," Politico, 29 June 2015, http://www.politico.com/story/2015/06/ted-cruz-gay-marriage-ruling-reaction-npr-interview-119559.

[566] Thomas Kaplan and Robert Pearjune, "Secrecy Surrounding Senate Health Bill Raises Alarms in Both Parties," *New York Times*, 15 June 2017.

[567] William Goldschlag and Dan Janison, "Stephen Miller on Ban: Trump's Authority 'Will not be Questioned,' " *Newsday*, 13 February 2017, http://www.newsday.com/long-island/politics/aide-on-ban-fight-trump-s-authority-will-not-be-questioned-1.13112408.

[568] Kevin Baker, "The Myth of the Smug Liberal," *New Republic*, 6 January 2016, https://newrepublic.com/article/139169/myth-smug-liberal.

member states did not acquiesce to Trump administration threats.[569] President Trump mocked commentators who criticized the overwhelming wealth of his cabinet members, explaining to a laughing audience at a rally that he just doesn't "want a poor person' running the economy."[570] Mysticism and escapism dominate pop culture in 2017 with metaphysical offerings such as *Stranger Things*, *The Good Place*, and *Falling Water*.[571] Democrats, too, continue to promote an irrational fear of Russia, when it is clear that both nations would benefit from cooperation and neither could "win" a nuclear war.[572] And Hillary Clinton and the Democratic National Committee continue to blame James Comey, sexism, and Russia for her pathetic campaign performance that most serious analysts blame on her record, her rhetoric, and her stubborn refusal to learn from the success of Bernie Sanders.[573] Thus, the American Corporate-Fascist system promotes all ten of Krueckel's Fascist traits in the individual.

And in the country where most Republicans support capital punishment, if the American Corporate-Fascist State chooses to

---

[569] Ben Evansky, "UN Ambassador Nikki Haley warns North Korea America Has 'Considerable Military Options,' " Fox News 5 July 2017.

[570] Jacob Pramuk, "President Donald Trump Says He Doesn't Want a Poor Person' to Run the U.S. Economy, CNBC, 22 June 2017, http://www.cnbc.com/2017/06/22/trump-i-just-dont-want-a-poor-person-running-the-economy.html.

[571] Spencer Kornhaber, "Pop Culture Is Having a Metaphysical Moment," *Atlantic*, 5 January 2017, https://www.theatlantic.com/entertainment/archive/2017/01/the-oa-stranger-things-westworld-metaphysical-moment-alternative-realities-tv/511808/.

[572] Doug Bandow, "What Russian Threat? Americans Shouldn't Be Running Scared of Moscow," *Forbes*, 3 May 2017, https://www.forbes.com/sites/dougbandow/2017/03/06/what-russian-threat-americans-shouldnt-be-running-scared-of-moscow/#4fecd11513c9.

[573] Matt Mackowiak, "Clinton Seeks Scapegoats for Her 2016 Debacle," *Washington Times* 3 May 2017, http://www.washingtontimes.com/news/2017/may/3/hillary-clinton-seeks-scapegoats-for-her-2016-deba/.

take action and exercise its authority to execute a citizen, individual rights are dismissed as weakness on crime. When the state of Arkansas discovered that its supply of the lethal injection ingredient midazolam would expire at the end of April 2017, the state scheduled an unprecedented eight executions for the middle of April. One of the condemned, Jason McGehee, asked for mercy based on a "dysfunctional" childhood in which McGehee's mother forced him to sleep outside for days and denied him food; his father executed two family pets in front of McGehee, but the jury convicted McGehee in 90 minutes and sentenced him to death.[574] A federal appeals court panel rejected arguments that the execution of McGehee and the several others was cruel because of the several recorded incidents of torturous deaths caused by similar injection protocols.[575] McGehee was not an individual to the powers that be in Arkansas or "The Republican Party, a party of law and order," that "must make clear in words and action that every human life matters,"[576] but somehow not McGehee; all they could see was an opportunity to wield the full violent force of the state against its own natural born citizen in the name of this "law and order" that was too vengeful and blind to see its own deadly hypocrisy.

The American Civil Liberties Union, however, continues to oppose the death penalty and champion individual rights. The ACLU website offers a guide to individual rights for download, including the following advice for interacting with police:

YOUR RIGHTS

---

[574] Barnini Chakraborty, "Arkansas Executions: Who's on Death Row?" *FoxNews*, 17 April 2017.
[575] "The Latest: Arkansas to Appeal State Court's Execution Stays," *Associated Press*, 17 April 2017.
[576] Barasso, Fallin, and Foxx, *Republican Platform 2016*, 39.

You have the right to remain silent. If you wish to exercise that right, say so out loud.

You have the right to refuse to consent to a search of yourself, your car or your home.

If you are not under arrest, you have the right to calmly leave. You have the right to a lawyer if you are arrested. Ask for one immediately.

Regardless of your immigration or citizenship status, you have constitutional rights.

YOUR RESPONSIBILITIES

Do stay calm and be polite.

Do not interfere with or obstruct the police.

Do not lie or give false documents.

Do prepare yourself and your family in case you are arrested.

Do remember the details of the encounter.

Do file a written complaint or call your local ACLU if you feel your rights have been violated.[577]

The increasing police presence and continuing impunity require special vigilance. We also would do well to imitate the righteous individuality of Sojourner Truth at her 1851 address to a women's convention in Akron, Ohio:

---

[577] "Know Your Rights: What to Do if You Are Stopped by Police, Immigration Agents, or the FBI," ACLU, 2017, https://www.aclu.org/know-your-rights/what-do-if-youre-stopped-police-immigration-agents-or-fbi.

Well, children, where there is so much racket there must be something out of kilter. I think that 'twixt the negroes of the South and the women at the North, all talking about rights, the white men will be in a fix pretty soon. But what's all this here talking about?

That man over there says that women need to be helped into carriages, and lifted over ditches, and to have the best place everywhere. Nobody ever helps me into carriages, or over mud-puddles, or gives me any best place! And ain't I a woman? Look at me! Look at my arm! I have ploughed and planted, and gathered into barns, and no man could head me! And ain't I a woman? I could work as much and eat as much as a man - when I could get it - and bear the lash as well! And ain't I a woman? I have borne thirteen children, and seen most all sold off to slavery, and when I cried out with my mother's grief, none but Jesus heard me! And ain't I a woman?

Then they talk about this thing in the head; what's this they call it? [member of audience whispers, "intellect"] That's it, honey. What's that got to do with women's rights or negroes' rights? If my cup won't hold but a pint, and yours holds a quart, wouldn't you be mean not to let me have my little half measure full?

Then that little man in black there, he says women can't have as much rights as men, 'cause Christ wasn't a woman! Where did your Christ come from? Where did your Christ come from? From God and a woman! Man had nothing to do with Him.

If the first woman God ever made was strong enough to turn the world upside down all alone, these women together ought to be able to turn it back, and get it right side up again! And now they is asking to do it, the men better let them.

The abolition and women's suffrage movements that Truth champions both came to eventual victory, but only with persistent and smart organizing all the way down at the level of the individual.

The Amendment and the Plan

"Society has claims on us all."
  —Jane Austen

"Corporations have no consciences…."
  —Justice John Paul Stevens

"I felt increasing pressure to say the war was winnable."
  —Ray Cline

If the problem with American-style Corporate-Fascism is the totalitarian regime that emerges from militarism, authoritarianism, nationalism, and expansionism at the service of capitalism, then what is the solution, and how might a constitutional amendment further our cause? Since the goal of capitalism is the accumulation of capital—money—to use to accumulate more money by any means possible, including corruption or bribery in order to create and modify markets that benefit the wealthiest and most powerful capitalists who regularly manipulate society, polity, and disregard humanity, then we should do something to constrain money within the norms of society. The non-profit political action group Move to Amend urges us to support an amendment that would overturn pro-corporate rulings in cases such as *Citizens United v. Federal Election Commission*, and instead "firmly establish that money is not speech, and that human beings, not corporations, are persons entitled to constitutional rights."[578]

---

[578] Move to Amend, "We the People, Not We the Corporations," Movetoamend.org, 2016.

On 30 January 2017, United States Representative Richard M. Nolan of Minnesota presented Joint Resolution 48: Proposing an amendment to the Constitution of the United States providing that the rights extended by the Constitution are the rights of natural persons only. As of 29 May 2017, the proposal enjoys 40 cosponsors; the text reads:

Section 1. [Artificial Entities Such as Corporations Do Not Have Constitutional Rights]

The rights protected by the Constitution of the United States are the rights of natural persons only.

Artificial entities established by the laws of any State, the United States, or any foreign state shall have no rights under this Constitution and are subject to regulation by the People, through Federal, State, or local law.

The privileges of artificial entities shall be determined by the People, through Federal, State, or local law, and shall not be construed to be inherent or inalienable.

Section 2. [Money is Not Free Speech]

Federal, State, and local government shall regulate, limit, or prohibit contributions and expenditures, including a candidate's own contributions and expenditures, to ensure that all citizens, regardless of their economic status, have access to the political process, and that no person gains, as a result of their money, substantially more access or ability to influence in any way the election of any candidate for public office or any ballot measure.

Federal, State, and local government shall require that any permissible contributions and expenditures be publicly disclosed.

The judiciary shall not construe the spending of money to influence elections to be speech under the First Amendment.

The plan to pass the amendment is ambitious but becoming more realistic in the present political climate, with only 20 to 30% of likely voters believing that "the country is heading in the right direction" in surveys from 2016 and 2017.[579] More specifically, a 2015 Bloomberg poll of over 1000 adults found that 78% viewed the *Citizens United* decision unfavorably; University of Chicago Professor David Strauss suggests that "*Citizens United* has become a symbol for what people perceive to be a much larger problem, which is the undue influence of wealth in politics."[580]

In addition, groups such as Refuse Fascism call for a more general strategy and tactics, beginning with an urgent call to action:

[1] Our single unifying mission must be to Drive Out the Trump/Pence Regime.

[2] We must manifest the power of NO! everywhere: on signs, billboards, walls, social media and the news. NO! In the Name of Humanity, We REFUSE to Accept a Fascist America must resound.

[3] Every outrage committed by this regime must be met with greater and greater resistance.

[4] We must ORGANIZE: working with all our creativity and determination toward the time when millions of people

---

[579] Rasmussen Reports, "Right Direction or Wrong Track," rasmussenreports.com, 29 May 2017.
[580] Cristian Farias, "Americans Agree on One Thing: Citizens United Is Terrible," *Huffington Post*, 29 September 2015.

can be moved to fill the streets of cities and towns day after day and night after night, declaring this whole regime illegitimate – Demanding, and Not Stopping, Until the Trump/Pence Regime Is Driven from Power.[581]

As Immanuel Kant wrote from Prussia eight years after the signing of the Declaration of Independence:

Here as elsewhere, when things are considered in broad perspective, a strange, unexpected pattern in human affairs reveals itself, one in which almost everything is paradoxical. A greater degree of civil freedom seems advantageous to a people's spiritual freedom; yet the former established impassable boundaries for the latter; conversely, a lesser degree of civil freedom provides enough room for all fully to expand their abilities. Thus, once nature has removed the hard shell from this kernel for which she has most fondly cared, namely, the inclination to and vocation for free thinking, the kernel gradually reacts on a people's mentality (whereby they become increasingly able to act freely), and it finally even influences the principles of government, which finds that it can profit by treating men, who are now more than machines, in accord with their dignity.

In our free-thinking dignity we must dismantle the Corporate-Fascist rule that oppresses democracy, and replace it with a new paradigm in which the economy operates within the needs of society and the principles of democracy.

---

[581] Refuse Fascism, "The Call to Action," refusefascism.org, 2017, https://refusefascism.org/the-call-to-action-drive-out-the-trumppence-regime/.

Acknowledgements

I would like to thank the inspiring activism, journalism, scholarship, rhetoric, and art of Janine Jackson, Seymour Hersh, Amy Goodman, Dennis Bernstein, Stefania Maurizi, Gore Vidal, Arundhati Roy, Upton Sinclair, Angela Davis, Cesar Chavez, and all of my students over the years.

About the Author

Eric Michael Moberg is a career educator, interdisciplinary researcher, and novelist who teaches rhetoric, business communication, and literature in Northern California and online.

His novels include:
> *Big Noise at the Funky Butt Jass club*
> *Cowboys and Scumbags*
> *End of Summer*

His monographs include:
> *Class War 2012*
> *Machiavelli was Wrong*
> *Adam Smith and Karl Marx Walk in to a Bar:*
> > *A Neo-Platonic Dialogue with Ayn Rand*

His children's books include:
> *My Mother Wears a White Lab Coat*
> *Red, White, and Blue Streak 1000*
> *So, You Want to be an Artist?*

His Academia page is available at:
https://sfsu.academia.edu/EricMoberg

and his Amazon page is available at:
https://www.amazon.com/s?ie=UTF8&page=1&rh=n%3A283155%2Cp_27%3AEric%20Moberg

and his Goodreads page is available at:
https://www.goodreads.com/author/show/4953962.Eric_Michael_Moberg